BEYOND BELIEF

Rethinking the Voice to Parliament

Beyond Belief

RETHINKING THE VOICE TO PARLIAMENT

EDITED BY

PETER KURTI & WARREN MUNDINE AO

Foreword by Senator Jacinta Nampijinpa Price

connorcourt

PUBLISHING

Published in 2022 by Connor Court Publishing Pty Ltd

Connor Court Publishing Pty Ltd
PO Box 7257
Redland Bay QLD 4165

sales@connorcourt.com
www.connorcourtpublishing.com.au

ISBN: 978-1-922815-28-6

Front Cover Design by Ian James

Printed in Australia

Dedicated to the first three Indigenous Voices to Parliament, to the Liberal Party of Australia that first heard the call for Indigenous representation, and to the future Indigenous generations that can now follow in their footsteps.

Neville Bonner
LP Federal 1971-1983

Hyacinth Tungutalum
CLP NT 1974-1977

Eric Deeral
CP Qld 1974-1977

My heart is heavy. I worry for my children and my grandchildren. I worry that what has proven to be a stable society, which now recognizes my people as equals, is about to be replaced. How dare you. I repeat, how dare you.

You told my people that your system was best. We have come to accept that. We have come to believe that. The dispossessed and despised adapted to your system. Now you say that you were wrong and that we were wrong to believe you.

Suddenly you are saying that what brought the country together, made it independent, ensured its defence, saw it through peace and war, and saw it through depression and prosperity – you are saying all this must go.

I cannot see the need for change. I cannot see how it will help my people. I cannot see how it will resolve the questions of land and access to land that trouble us.

Fellow Australians, what is most hurtful is that after all we have learned together, after subjugating us and then freeing us, once again you are telling us that you know better.

How dare you. How dare you!

Neville Bonner

1998 Constitutional Convention on an Australian Republic

CONTENTS

The Uluru Statement from the Heart   ix

Foreword
Senator Jacinta Nampijinpa Price   xi

Introduction
On reconsidering the Voice to Parliament   1

1   The Voice: A Plea to Reconsider
     Tony Abbott   5

2   The Voice: Self-determination or separatism?
     Anthony Dillon   13

3   The Voice: Beyond Belief?
     Janet Albrechtsen   27

4   Constitutional Change by Stealth
     Chris Merritt   45

5   What Conservative Voice supporters get Wrong about
     Constitutional Recognition
     Bernard Samuelson   57

6   The Indigenous Voice does Not Speak for Country
     Nyunggai Warren Mundine   73

7   Head over Heart: The Legal, Democratic and Practical
     Problems raised by the Uluru Statement
     Amanda Stoker   89

8   It's OK for liberals (and anyone else) to say 'No' to indigenous recognition in the Constitution
Scott Prasser   105

9   Indigenous Social Justice won't be solved with Poetic Justice
Neenah Gray   119

10   The Voice: What are We Being Asked to Decide?
Caroline Di Russo   129

11   Constitutional Recognition is Not Necessary for Integration – Australia's Migrant Story tells us so
Rocco Loiacono   141

12   The Voice in the Light of the Western Intellectual Tradition
Henry Ergas   153

Contributors   171

The Uluru Statement from the Heart

We, gathered at the 2017 National Constitutional Convention, coming from all points of the southern sky, make this statement from the heart:

Our Aboriginal and Torres Strait Islander tribes were the first sovereign Nations of the Australian continent and its adjacent islands, and possessed it under our own laws and customs. This our ancestors did, according to the reckoning of our culture, from the Creation, according to the common law from 'time immemorial', and according to science more than 60,000 years ago.

This sovereignty is a spiritual notion: the ancestral tie between the land, or 'mother nature', and the Aboriginal and Torres Strait Islander peoples who were born therefrom, remain attached thereto, and must one day return thither to be united with our ancestors. This link is the basis of the ownership of the soil, or better, of sovereignty. It has never been ceded or extinguished, and co-exists with the sovereignty of the Crown.

How could it be otherwise? That peoples possessed a land for sixty millennia and this sacred link disappears from world history in merely the last two hundred years?

With substantive constitutional change and structural reform, we believe this ancient sovereignty can shine through as a fuller expression of Australia's nationhood.

Proportionally, we are the most incarcerated people on the planet. We are not an innately criminal people. Our children are aliened from their families at unprecedented rates. This cannot be because we have no love for them.

And our youth languish in detention in obscene numbers. They should be our hope for the future.

These dimensions of our crisis tell plainly the structural nature of our problem. This is the torment of our powerlessness.

We seek constitutional reforms to empower our people and take a rightful place in our own country. When we have power over our destiny our children will flourish. They will walk in two worlds and their culture will be a gift to their country.

We call for the establishment of a First Nations Voice enshrined in the Constitution.

Makarrata is the culmination of our agenda: the coming together after a struggle. It captures our aspirations for a fair and truthful relationship with the people of Australia and a better future for our children based on justice and self-determination.

We seek a Makarrata Commission to supervise a process of agreement-making between governments and First Nations and truth-telling about our history.

In 1967 we were counted, in 2017 we seek to be heard. We leave base camp and start our trek across this vast country. We invite you to walk with us in a movement of the Australian people for a better future.

FOREWORD

THE VOICE SOUNDS TOO GOOD TO BE TRUE

Senator Jacinta Nampijinpa Price

There is one phrase that sums up Indigenous affairs: *the road to hell is paved with good intentions.*

Decades of well-intentioned federal and state territory policy have failed to improve the lives of Australia's most disadvantaged first peoples. "Self-determination" has produced the opposite amid the violence, squalor and despair in Aboriginal communities of rural and remote Australia.

The way forward should be to work hard to peel back layers of failed policy to get to the root of the demise of marginalised Aboriginal Australia. Instead, governments have compounded the failure in two ways.

The first is by further marginalising the voiceless and vulnerable.

The second way is by empowering a self-serving Indigenous "industry" that seeks to maintain its relevance.

It is this industry – comprising Aboriginal services providers, bureaucrats, academics, and politicians – that demands that its voice be constitutionally recognised under the false pretence that doing so will provide all of the answers to past failures and simultaneously close the gap.

Sounds too good to be true? Well it is.

If recognition of Indigenous people in our founding governing charter had been done right, it could have helped reconcile black and white Australia.

But the globally unprecedented Voice proposal, to which the Uluru Statement gave rise, will divide Australia along racial lines, entrench indigenous separatism, and constitutionally enshrine the idea that Aboriginal people are perpetual victims forever in need of special measures.

There are many reasons why Australians should stand up and say 'No' to the Indigenous Voice to parliament and this book outlines those reasons. I applauded the courage and conviction of all the contributors willing to publicly declare their position. Too few Australians are prepared to air their doubts in this woke age of social media pile-ons and cancellations.

The fallacy of the 'Yes' case is that those who say 'No' are, at best, standing in the way of Reconciliation. These essays show why it is important for the Australian people to hear the other side of a debate that is critical to both the future of Indigenous policy and the operation of Australia's national parliament and government.

I therefore applaud Peter Kurti and Warren Mundine for compiling this collection that sets out the 'No' case – a case that, frankly, no one else is making, but which needs to be heard in the interests of all Australians.

INTRODUCTION

ON RECONSIDERING THE VOICE TO PARLIAMENT

Advocates for an Aboriginal and Torres Strait Islander First Nations Voice to the Commonwealth Parliament have long argued that only by creation of such a body can it be possible to achieve full, effective, and lasting reconciliation with Indigenous Australians.

When Prime Minister Anthony Albanese addressed the Garma Festival in July 2022, just weeks after winning an election, he committed his government to holding a referendum in its first term on the idea of enshrining a Voice to parliament in the Australian Constitution.

Changing the Constitution is not easy, which is just as its framers intended. Indeed, in the 121 years since Federation, only eight of the 44 attempts to change the Constitution have succeeded. Even so, many advocates for the Voice appear to suppose that success for this attempt at constitutional amendment is inevitable, imagining that the unquestionable good will, which all Australians bear towards their Indigenous sisters and brothers, will be sufficient to win popular support for adjusting the nation's founding document.

However, by the time of writing, in the latter part of 2022, there is mounting evidence to indicate that while the Australian public is aware of the proposed referendum, majority support for a move to tamper with the Constitution is far from assured. Proponents of the Voice argue that the proposed adjustment to the Constitution is very modest and will not interfere with the processes of Australian parliamentary democracy; but the electorate does not appear to be convinced and remains sceptical.

For one thing, details about what the Voice would actually look like, and how it would function, are vanishingly thin. For another, the 2022 federal election saw 11 Indigenous people elected to the Commonwealth Parliament, representing a substantial and talented representation of the country's Indigenous population. Doesn't this represent the best possible Indigenous 'voice' to the Commonwealth Parliament?

Proponents of the Voice argue that Australia can only pay full and proper respect to the country's history by altering the Constitution. However, the Constitution was never intended to provide a historical synopsis of the continent. As the founding document of Australia, the Constitution is an agreement struck between former colonies to create a nation in which powers are distributed between the states and the new Commonwealth.

Our purpose in compiling this collection of essays is to restore some balance to the arguments being advanced in the referendum campaign, and to show that there are many good and compelling reasons to be sceptical about the move to enshrine a Voice to parliament in the Constitution.

Each of the contributors was invited to present their own reasons why Australians should decline to support the referendum. Some of these reasons are concerned with points of constitutional law; others express concern about the likely impact of a constitutionally enshrined Voice on Australia's highly cohesive society. The final chapter, by Henry Ergas, is a thorough survey of the issues surrounding constitutional amendment which sets the matter in the broader historical context of the Western political and intellectual tradition.

The chapters can be read in any order and none presuppose that others have been read first. While there is some overlap in the topics covered, the arguments they present here demonstrate clearly not only that the legal and constitutional reasons for saying 'No' are complex, subtle, and compelling, but that the creation of a Voice threatens not so much to unite the country as to divide it.

In particular, a number of the contributors subject Anthony Albanese's three-point 'Garma Statement' to careful scrutiny. Despite being presented as merely a modest amendment, they argue that it would make a fundamental alteration to the processes of government by giving to members of the Voice an extra say on any act – or omission – of the Commonwealth government which relates to Indigenous people. This, in turn, they argue, threatens to introduce racial division to the governing of Australia, one of the world's most successful multi-racial and multi-cultural societies.

No attempt is made in this collection to ignore the persisting and deeply troubling gap between Indigenous and non-Indigenous Australians which successive governments have attempted, without great success, to close. The arguments put forward in these essays for saying 'No' emphasise the political and moral imperative of addressing this gap; but they confront head on the reality that constitutional amendment can be little more than a superficial gesture which does nothing to address the pressing social deprivation, compounded by domestic violence and substance abuse, endured by many Indigenous Australians.

It will, of course, be for the Australian people to decide whether or not enshrining the Voice in the Constitution promises to unite us or divide us. It will also be for them to judge the wisdom of inserting a race-based body which gives priority to just one section of the community in our parliamentary democracy thereby changing our established system of government.

We commend this collection of essays to the Australian public in the hope not only that it will contribute to a more informed debate about the referendum proposal but that it will also add weight to the reasons for declining to make such a change to the Constitution.

Although proponents of the Voice promise that it will somehow deliver rich results for our nation, the reality is that it is likely not only to deliver little but to compound disaffection and division. Every Australian needs to weigh carefully the arguments in this collection which highlight the risk we run by amending the nation's Constitution for a purpose that is not specified and a reason that remains unclear.

Peter Kurti and Nyunggai Warren Mundine

Sydney

November 2022

1

THE VOICE: A PLEA TO RECONSIDER
Tony Abbott

It's wrong in principle and bad in practice, so let's not put-back reconciliation with a referendum that fails.

I support recognising Indigenous people in the constitution but only if it's done in ways that don't damage our system of government and don't compromise our national unity. Done well, recognition would complete our consitution rather than change it. Done badly, recognition would entrench race-based separatism and make the business of government even harder than it currently is.

As shown by the British government's injunction to Governor Phillip to "live in amity" with the original inhabitants, there has always been a degree of official goodwill towards the first Australians. The fact that this has now percolated far beyond high-minded documents to become the overwhelming instinct of the entire Australian people shows how far we've come in two centuries. It may indeed be simple "good manners", as Prime Minister Anthony Albanese says, to want to acknowledge generously in our nation's founding document the original inhabitants who were most regrettably (given the prejudices of the 1890s) overlooked when it was first instituted. Yet it would be a dreadful mistake for an abundance of goodwill to propel changing the constitution without careful regard for its consequences; because constitutional change is "for keeps" in a way that mere policy change or legislative change is not.

As leader of the opposition, and then as prime minister, I fully supported the principle of constitutional recognition that John Howard had first pledged in the lead-up to the 2007 election and that's been bi-partisan policy ever since. I didn't support the Gillard-era proposal that section 51(xxvi) of the constitution might be changed to replace the Commonwealth parliament's "race power" with a power to make laws "for the benefit" of Indigenous people because this would have invited the High Court to adjudicate on the actual beneficence of any such law.

Seeking an alternative, in July 2015, I jointly chaired, with the then opposition leader, a round table of about 40 Indigenous leaders to chart a process that might lead to a better proposal. The plan that emerged was to have a series of consultations, not just among Indigenous people, but among the wider community too (because the constitution belongs to everyone) in the hope of putting to the people a proposal that might readily succeed on the fiftieth anniversary of the successful 1967 referendum to give the Commonwealth power to make laws for Indigenous people.

Unfortunately, it was only the Indigenous half of that consultation process that ultimately took place under my successor. This culminated in the 2017 Uluḻu Statement from the Heart that called for so much more than just constitutional recognition. It sought an Indigenous "voice to parliament" in order to give Indigenous people much more say on the workings of government; as well as treaties between the Australian government and so-called "First Nation" groups; plus a "truth telling" commission to uncover and to publicise further injustices that Indigenous people had suffered.

In other words, the original, all-but-universally-supported proposal to recognise Indigenous people in the constitution had morphed (or run off the rails even) into a much larger proposal for a series of ongoing changes that were not only supposed to make governance more responsive to Indigenous people but to change the understanding of Australian history. At least, that's what the then-Prime Minister Malcolm Turnbull judged had taken place when he declined to support the voice on the grounds that it would amount to a third chamber of the parliament. Although Turnbull says that he has changed his mind and now supports the voice, he still admits that it would be "an enormous change to the way our parliamentary system works".

At the recent Garma festival, Anthony Albanese called for the constitution to be amended in three specific respects: first, that there should be enshrined "a body, to be called the Aboriginal and Torres Strait Islander Voice"; second, that this Voice would make representations to both the parliament and to the executive government "on matters relating to" Indigenous peoples; and third, that this Voice's "composition, functions, powers and procedures" would be determined by the parliament.

In other words, should this proposal succeed, there would have to be a Voice; it would have to be listened to; and its powers and functions could be as wide as a parliament might make them. Despite insisting that the Voice would be merely advisory, as the PM subsequently admitted, it would have to be a very "brave" parliament and government that didn't accept its advice.

In my judgment, there are four massive issues with this concept of Indigenous recognition-by-way-of-a-Voice.

First, it's a race based-body comprising only Indigenous people. Unless the government is to nominate, or the parliament is to select, the members of the Voice, there would presumably have to be a race-based electoral roll determining who could stand for election and who could vote for the Voice's members. This would give Indigenous people two votes: first, like everyone else, a vote for the parliament itself; and second, in a right that's uniquely theirs, a vote for the Voice.

If governments were in the habit of making decisions for Indigenous people without their input, or if the parliament were devoid of Indigenous representation, there might at least be an argument for such a special Indigenous body. As it's happened though, constitutionally entrenching a separate Indigenous Voice when there are already eleven individual Indigenous voices in the parliament, and when there's arguably "analysis paralysis" from a surfeit of Indigenous consultation mechanisms already, is a pretty strange way to eliminate racism from our constitution and from our institutional arrangements.

Second, it would vastly complicate the difficulties of getting legislation passed and anything done. If the Voice chooses to have a view on anything-at-all that touches Indigenous people, that view would have to be taken very seriously by government; indeed, on the prime minister's view, it would be a veto in fact, if not in theory.

Third, in the event that an Indigenous person or entity were aggrieved by a government that failed to give the Voice a chance to make representations on any issue, or that then ignored it, there could readily be an application to the High Court to rule that the constitution had been breached. This is the likely consequence of importing into the constitution such a vague-yet-portentous concept as a "Voice" (as opposed to one described as an advisory body or a commission) – especially one that's said to be the means of putting an end to centuries of marginalisation. At the very least, the existence of a Voice could import further delay into the finalisation of legislation or decision-making as it's given adequate time to investigate and come to its conclusions.

Fourth, the whole point of Indigenous recognition is to address a gap in what's otherwise been an admirable constitution and, in so doing, to help to complete the reconciliation of Indigenous people with modern Australia. There could hardly be a greater set back to reconciliation than a referendum that fails. Yet that is the likelihood – at least based on the record of previous attempts to change the constitution – in the absence of substantial bi-partisan support.

Although the Coalition's Indigenous affairs shadow minister has previously been an in-principle supporter of a Voice (and accompanied the Prime Minister to Garma), the new Coalition senator for the Northern Territory, the proud "Celtic Warlpiri Australian" woman, Jacinta Price, has expressed deep scepticism about a proposal with so much of the detail thus far omitted, with so much potential for ineffective posturing, and that defines people by racial heritage.

The only way the current proposal could succeed would be by playing to Australians' unease over Indigenous dispossession and desire to be on "the right side of history". Even so, were figures such as Price and the former ALP national president and later Liberal candidate, Warren Mundine, to figure prominently in any "no" campaign, it's hard to see the voice winning over a majority of the people plus a majority of the states.

My strong hope is that the government might reconsider the wisdom of putting a proposal that's problematic in principle, doubtful in practice, and probably doomed to fail. It would be a pity, though, were the whole bid for constitutional recognition to founder because it had become a proposal pushed by activists who sought too much. In my judgment, there is a proposal that could succeed because it passes the test of successful constitution-making: namely, having something for everyone but not too much for anyone.

On quite a few occasions as prime minister, including at a "recognise" dinner in December 2014, I described Australia as having "an Indigenous heritage, a British foundation, and a multi-cultural character". These days, because multi-culturalism is a contested concept, I'd prefer to substitute the term "immigrant character". My inclination, back then, depending on how the consultations had developed, would have been to propose an amendment to the constitutional preamble, so that it would henceforth read "Whereas the people....humbly relying on the blessing of Almighty God, have agreed to unite in one indissoluble Federal Commonwealth, *with an Indigenous heritage, a British foundation, and an immigrant character*, under the Crown....and under the Constitution hereby established".

The italicised amendment would add words that were self-evidently true; that had the potential to speak to everyone, whether descended from Indigenous people or the latest arrival; that provided a good short-hand description of Australia; and that could hardly be mischievously judicially mis-applied to interfere with the processes of governing. It also had the advantage, I thought, of building on Noel Pearson's concept of the "pillars" on which modern Australia rests; with the degree of emphasis that might be given to each one of them a matter for individual choice.

It would actually be the strength of such a proposal that it would be symbolic change only; because any change that went beyond that would inevitably involve much more than recognition itself and become a change to the way Australia is governed. That's precisely the current difficulty: the quest for recognition has evolved into a demand for this entirely novel governmental entity that, it's implausibly claimed, would both make a big difference and yet be no big deal; combined with the palpably false claim that Indigenous people currently have no say over governmental decisions that affect them.

Of itself, the change I had in mind would not solve the issues bedevilling Indigenous Australia. It would still be up to the wisdom of government and the initiative of individuals to raise Indigenous life expectancy, to increase educational attainments and to boost employment prospects.

But of itself, neither is grafting an Indigenous voice onto the parliament going to get the kids to school, the adults to work, and the ordinary law of the land applied in remote communities. Indeed, there's a paradox here: at the very time when the Prime Minister says that a constitutionally entrenched Indigenous voice is the government's highest first term priority, the government is seeking to pass legislation abolishing the cashless debit card against the express wishes of several key Indigenous leaders in the communities where it's helped to reduce alcohol-fuelled violence.

Especially if a Voice turns out to be largely the preserve of activists from the big cities, it's far more likely to be a permanent echo chamber for grievance than a mechanism for reconciliation and a better life for Indigenous people. The likely result won't be one Australian nation but a country where the descendants of the original inhabitants have a privileged position over everyone else whose local roots go back no further than 1788.

I can understand why Indigenous leaders would want constitutional change to go beyond the symbolic in order to produce better outcomes for their own people; and hence the call for their own unique voice to which the parliament should defer. But better outcomes are ultimately the product of better attitudes; and these are more likely to be engendered by a generous acknowledgment of all the elements that have made modern Australia such a special place than by creating yet more elements of government based on Indigenous ancestry.

If against the better judgment of many who have studied the voice proposal as it currently stands, it should prevail at a referendum and be incorporated into the constitution, it will be the duty of every Australian to make the most of the new situation. Against expectation, perhaps it would turn out to be the kind of forum where Indigenous people of goodwill respectfully debate the issues that particularly impact them – and not a forum for point-scoring, grand-standing and grievance-mongering; perhaps it could, after all, become the kind of forum that all Australians might wish our parliament to be. We can but hope.

It's just that, based on what we know, the voice is wrong in principle, almost sure to be bad in practice, and unlikely to succeed in any referendum. If it fails, reconciliation is set back. If it succeeds, our country is permanently divided by race. Hence the fundamental question: why further consider something that would leave us worse off whichever way it goes?

2

THE VOICE:
SELF-DETERMINATION OR SEPARATISM?

Anthony Dillon

Introduction

Some of what I write in this chapter I have expressed in recent times in the popular news media when discussing the Indigenous voice to parliament as mentioned in the Uluru Statement from the Heart (see page ix and hereafter referred to as 'the Voice' with a capital 'V'). In this chapter, I have taken a step back to focus on what I believe is a fundamental flaw of the Voice. This is something that I have not written about before.

In the first part of the chapter, I discuss this fundamental flaw of the Voice (separatism) and then follow with some questions we should ask if the Voice does get up. I do this because, regardless of its perceived failings, there is a chance that the Voice might get up. Finally, I offer some advice for those opposing the Voice, given that their actions could bring about the opposite of what they want if they are not too careful.

Basically, I am not convinced that the Voice will make any practical difference to Aboriginal people. I am not outright opposing it, but at present, given the lack of detail, I am not convinced of its merits. If a clear explanation of how Aboriginal people will benefit in any practical way is presented, then I will consider it carefully. I am of a similar mindset to Aboriginal leader Pat Turner who was reported in *The Australian* newspaper as saying that she would like to see "some meat on the bones." However, I am doubtful that anything could be said to convince me of the Voice's merits because, from what I can see, its premise is fundamentally flawed.

The Sin of Separatism

New generation, same bad old idea

Although the idea of the Voice has only been around for a few years, it is the latest manifestation of an idea that has been popular in Aboriginal affairs for much longer; in fact, I believe it rules Aboriginal affairs. This idea is the belief that Aboriginal people are a collective group who are fundamentally different to non-Aboriginal people; implicit in this idea is that Aboriginal people are all very much alike. This unquestioned belief in fundamental difference is at the root of all problems facing Aboriginal people today.

There are a couple of corollaries to the idea of Aboriginal difference. First, it is assumed that the normal processes for communication between government and most Australians are ineffective where Aboriginal people are concerned. Second, it is assumed that Aboriginal people's fundamental needs are very different from other Australians and therefore they alone are best placed to understand and help Aboriginal people. All this of course sets the scene for preferencing Aboriginal people only for advising on Aboriginal affairs, which essentially, is what the Voice is all about.

I strongly disagree with the premise that Aboriginal people are a homogenous group vastly different from non-Aboriginal people.

14

As I have been saying for more than two decades, the common-alities between the two groups far outweigh any differences. It is for this reason that I believe that the Voice will not succeed in improving the lives of Aboriginal people. However, as I have said before when challenging the many proposed solutions to helping Aboriginal people, if the Voice does make a practical difference, then I will gladly admit I was wrong; but if I am right, we will need to get on with doing what we know works to improve the health and wellbeing of Aboriginal people. I am of course referring to education and employment (E&E), which, of course, is what works for non-Aboriginal people too. Interestingly, the main proponents of the Voice (Aboriginal leaders whom I greatly respect, even if I don't always agree with them), have achieved what they have be-cause of E&E.

Before continuing, it is worth noting, lest I be accused of offering simplistic solutions, that achieving E&E is not always easy. One's circumstances play an important part. Many successful Aboriginal people were either born into circumstances that had opportuni-ties or were able to escape bad circumstances and go where the opportunities were. For those who can't easily escape the environ-ments that seem cut off from modern society, this, I believe, will be our greatest challenge. Does the voice have a plan to address this challenge?

The deception of self-determination

At this stage, it seems that the Voice is about providing advice to parliament on matters affecting Aboriginal people. As I have said, it presupposes a vast difference between Aboriginal people and non-Aboriginal people.

If the Voice does go ahead, then I suspect that the advice given to parliament will be that Aboriginal people are the preferred service providers and minders for Aboriginal people. This will happen under the banner of 'self-determination.' In sum, my main argument against the Voice, is that I believe it is an expression of self-determination. But surely self-determination is a good thing? Isn't it? Well it depends how you define self-determination. The devil is in the detail.

Platitudes like "Aboriginal people taking care of Aboriginal affairs" sound lovely and give many those warm fuzzy feelings. Now, I don't outright reject the idea of Aboriginal people providing services to Aboriginal people, nor do I outright oppose having warm fuzzy feelings. I have seen far too many good Aboriginal services to make a blanket statement and dismiss any Aboriginal service that provides services to Aboriginal people. If an Aboriginal service is good, then I am happy for Aboriginal people to use it. I do have a problem however, when Aboriginal people are told that using this service is preferable to using mainstream services. The Aboriginal industry, in its quest to maintain relevance, encourages Aboriginal people to use Aboriginal services on the basis, first, that only Aboriginal people can fully understand and help Aboriginal people; and, second, it is an expression of self-determination. It is this last point that I want to discuss in greater depth.

If there is any doubt that the Voice has not been linked closely to the concept of self-determination, consider this statement from the Royal Australian College of General Practitioners: "As a medical organisation, the RACGP values the Uluru Statement as pathway to self-determination and, as such, a strong contributor to better health and wellbeing." Back in 2014, Aboriginal leader, the late Sol Bellear, wrote: "If we want to shift Aboriginal disadvantage, then self-determination is the only way to achieve that." Are these two statements correct?

Two definitions of self-determination

Self-determination can be good, depending on what definition you are using. It can either be defined at the level of the individual or at the group level. I do believe that self-determination is a good principle at the individual level, but not so at the group level.

At the individual level, it means an individual making decisions or taking actions that impact positively on the individual directly or indirectly. For example, if I choose to go to the gym and adopt a healthy diet, that is self-determination. I may seek advice or assistance from those more qualified than me or from outside my cultural group. This is still individual self-determination.

At the group or collective level, self-determination can be thought of as members of a group looking after each other. On the 'Creative Spirits' webpage, self-determination is described as Aboriginal people taking care of their own affairs. It has been popular rhetoric in Aboriginal affairs for many years. In 2016, the then chairman of the National Aboriginal Community Controlled Health Organisation, Matthew Cooke, remarked:

> Now more than ever, self-determination must feature front and centre. It is imperative that Aboriginal communities and indigenous controlled medical services are empowered to develop and run programs for Aboriginal people that are culturally appropriate and reach those who desperately need support. We know it's the only model that works.

At the group level, self-determination is promoted as being about Aboriginal people using Aboriginal services. So for example, if an Aboriginal person gets help from an Aboriginal health service, that is considered self-determination. If the same person gets help from a non-Aboriginal health service, that is not considered self-determination, and hence not looked on favourably.

Collective self-determination = separatism

While having Indigenous people taking care of their own affairs (in the collective sense and not the individual sense) is promoted as self-determination, I believe it is actually separatism. Perhaps the words of Martin Luther King Jr. (MLK) spoken back in 1968 are relevant here:

> Since we are Americans, the solution to our problems will not come through seeking to build a separate black nation, but by finding the creative minority of the concerned from the ofttimes apathetic, and together moving toward that colorless power that we all need for security and justice.

Notice how MLK saw himself as an American. He certainly acknowledged his African roots, but he still saw himself and others with African ancestry as American. A little bit closer to home, Aboriginal politician, Alison Anderson, has stated:

> We Indigenous people need to be more like other Australians. I do not mean we should abandon our beliefs or our language but, like dozens of other cultures in Australia, we must learn to combine our own identities with participation in the broader society. That will not weaken us. It will make us stronger in who we are. To preserve the old ways, we must embrace the new ones.

I think it is fine that groups such as families or organisations, look within their group when seeking to address their needs where they are capable of doing so and wish to do so. But this is feasible, only if group members share a set of common values, goals, interests, or needs that creates a degree of bonding, cohesion, commitment, and unity between them and that distinguishes them from other groups. However, I don't believe this is the case for Aboriginal Australians. Nor is it the case for non-Aboriginal Australians. When selecting service providers for a non-Aboriginal community, whether it be a teacher, a politician, doctor, or sales assistant, most Aussies assess the service provider on their competence and not their colour. I believe most Aboriginal Australians think the same way. I am sure those who make their living from cross-cultural consultancies would disagree with me.

Those with the loudest voices may try to convince us that Aboriginal Australians function like one big family or organisation where members are alike but different to other Australians. However, Aboriginal Australians are diverse in their thinking, preferences, and individual circumstances. In this regard, they are no different to other Australians.

For some small communities where traditional customs, beliefs, and practices are adhered to, there may be some homogeneity among community members. However, to extrapolate from this and assert the homogeneity of the Indigenous race as a whole is untenable. And where small homogenous groups of Aboriginal people exist, they have the right to access the best quality services, just like other Australians. Some of these services may be Aboriginal and some may not. It is access to quality services that can meet the needs of the people that is the most important factor.

How well has separatism worked?

How well has the self-determination approach worked for Aboriginal Australians? Alison Anderson has stated: "The idea that separate development was the answer provided hope for many and jobs for an increasingly powerful few. However, it has failed." Noting the failure of the self-determination paradigm, Aboriginal commentator, Wesley Aird, wrote: "It is about time Indigenous Australians had access to the same level of sophistication instead of being relegated to 'culturally-appropriate service'."

Now, I am not opposed to Aboriginal Australians accessing services that are managed by Aboriginal Australians, if the service providers are competent (and colour is not a requirement for com-

19

petence in my opinion). Indeed, I have been privileged to know some outstanding Aboriginal service providers. Furthermore, the people seeking services should have a free choice and not feel compelled to access only those services with the Aboriginal brand label. Individuals having a choice is real self-determination. A distinguishing feature of these outstanding Aboriginal service providers' attitude and work ethic, is that like Alison Anderson, they "see people. Not categories, divisions, or races."

Separatism is a mindset that has failed, and can only ever fail, for Aboriginal Australians, and with tragic consequences. Not only is separatism founded on the mistruth that Aboriginal people are fundamentally different from non-Aboriginal people, but the separatist paradigm runs the risk of generating differences that don't exist. This can happen as people who identify as Aboriginal suddenly start behaving in ways or adopt attitudes that validate their claim of Aboriginality (for example, declaring, "I'm upset by Australia Day" or "I need a culturally safe space"). We observe this behaviour, and then government and organisations rush to generate policies in response—the Voice, for example.

We are all in this together, so let's start working together. More will be achieved with an 'us' mentality rather than the 'us and them' mentality which has dominated Aboriginal affairs for far too long. I am suggesting that instead of being concerned when 'non-Aboriginal people help Aboriginal people', simply see it as 'Australians helping Australians.'

Why the Voice might get up and what questions we should ask if it does

Based on the public responses I've seen, which, admittedly, have mostly been in a few 'right-leaning' media outlets, I don't think the Voice has much chance of getting up. However, while many people are deeply concerned about the plight of Aboriginal Australians, many are very emotional in their assessment of events and are guided by ideologies rather than cold facts. They will be easily impressed with the Voice.

One strong motivator for why many will likely vote for the Voice at a referendum is because a vote against the Voice will be framed as a vote against Aboriginal people and a vote for racism; and of course, nobody wants to be seen as a racist. All I am saying is, let's not assume that the Voice has no chance—stranger things have happened.

What follows are concerns I have if the Voice does get up. Perhaps these concerns are redundant, but I raise them based on the lack of clarity about the Voice and the Uluru Statement from the Heart more generally.

- What will the composition of members of the Voice committee be? If it is too few in number, there risks being a bias in views and priorities. If the number is too large, there are likely to be too many disagreements, assuming there is a mix of progressive and conservative voices.
- Greg Craven in *The Australian* raises some important concerns: "How is the voice chosen? Elected or appointed? Who is eligible to serve? What legislation is scrutinised? Is executive action examined? What are the grounds of scrutiny? What are its powers? How is it funded? How is it resourced?" These are sensible questions.
- While a focus on symbolic gestures is fine, this should not be at the expense of focusing on priorities like housing, health, employment, education, and safe communities. However, I suspect the focus will be on the easier task, that is, on symbolic gestures.

Are architects of the Voice going to tell us what their priorities are?

- In recent times, many institutions are tripping over themselves to make workplaces and public places, 'culturally safe.' With the Voice, will we see more of this? Is there a 'slippery slope' argument applicable here? Will organisations, businesses, and schools adopt an equivalent of a Voice. I notice that while acknowledgement of country was once confined to public meetings and special gatherings, it is now creeping into other areas of life (e.g., such as announcements on trains).

- What formal processes will exist for criticism, amendment, of providing any feedback regarding the Voice? Or will the Voice be an untouchable entity? This is what our ABC is like; while it can be criticised, it seems to be inviolable. We need to ensure, that the Voice can be questioned, challenged, and, if necessary, abolished.

- Most importantly, when will we see an action plan that details how having the Voice will help Aboriginal people in any practical way? What does the voice enable in the way of helping Aboriginal people, that cannot be done now?

In their zeal to see that the Voice does not get up, those who oppose it run the risk of trying too hard. Some of those opposing the Voice have suggested that it is somehow creating two different laws, with some calling it apartheid. If the Voice does get up, while I believe it will be ineffective, I don't think it will create two Australias. To use these ideas as arguments against the Voice, I believe runs the risk of pushing people towards a yes vote at referendum. It seems a tad alarmist to me.

The proposed referendum question, as reported by the ABC, is: "Do you support an alteration to the constitution that establishes an Aboriginal and Torres Strait Islander Voice?" I think a question of this nature, and the inability of proponents of the Voice thus far to articulate how it will help Aboriginal people in any practical way, is enough to convince a majority to vote against it.

Conclusion

An ABC website reports that a referendum could occur as early as May 2023. For the key Aboriginal advocates of the Voice who are leading the way, I suggest they use their own voice in the interim. They are all high achievers themselves and good role models for all Australians. They live in safe and comfortable homes, earn a good income, and know where their next meal is coming from. Perhaps they can give a statement from their hearts of how they have achieved success without the parliamentary voice. I'm guessing they would start with something like "I got an education, worked hard, didn't keep myself separate from other Australians ..."

At the time of writing this chapter, I had the great pleasure of attending Senator Jacinta Price's maiden speech in Parliament. It was a stellar speech. She spoke of injustices against Aboriginal people. Her passion in speaking out on these injustices, springs from personal experience; in particular, violence within her extended family and community. She has, in effect, carried the torch handed to her by her mother, Bess. Very early in my 'on-the-ground' experience in Aboriginal affairs, Bess Price, with her husband, Dave, were doing their best to provide a voice for the voiceless—Bess' family and other community members for whom violence is so common that it has become normalised.

While violence is violence, the Aboriginal experience is often different to the non-Aboriginal experience. Where there is a white perpetrator, there is usually no shortage of virtue-signalling activists busting themselves to give a voice to the victims and a condemnation of the perpetrators. But where the perpetrator is Aboriginal, political laryngitis takes hold and there is silence.

I wish to echo what Jacinta said in her maiden speech and at the celebratory gathering afterwards: as a priority, we should be giving a voice to the Aboriginal victims of violence now. There are victims who are without a voice because they are too terrified to speak out for fear of payback; or heaven forbid, fear that the perpetrators (often a close relative or partner) will be thrown in prison; or even sadder, they have become so desensitised to the crime they are subjected to that it doesn't occur to them that, as Australian citizens, they are entitled to protection. These are the people who need a voice—but not necessarily the Voice.

So why do these Aboriginal victims of violence not need the Voice? There already are laws and processes in place to ensure Aboriginal communities are safe and victims and perpetrators of violence are responded to accordingly when it does happen. What is missing, is backbone.

In order to help Aboriginal people most effectively, we don't need the Voice or other parts of the Uluru Statement. Rather, we need government, the public, media, journalists, leaders, and the justice system, to recognise that Aboriginal people are Australian citizens, and therefore have the same rights as other Australians. And of course, recognising these rights needs to be matched with resourcing people and communities, and educating the people about personal responsibility. We know the problems, the good will is there; let's use *our* voices now, to make it happen.

Suggested reading

Wesley Aird, "Closing the Aboriginal gap is not socially just", in Gary Johns (ed.), *Right social justice*, (Redland Bay, QLD: Connor Court, 2013).

Alison Anderson, "Real education, real jobs", in R. Craven, A. Dillon, & N. Parbury, (eds.), *In black & white: Australians All at the crossroads*, (Redland Bay, QLD: Connor Court, 2013).

Sol Bellear, "The case for Indigenous self-determination", *The Drum*, (21 October 2013).

"Principles of self-determination", *Creative Spirits* (17 June 2021).

3

THE VOICE: BEYOND BELIEF?

Janet Albrechtsen

PART 1

Analysing the 'Albanese Amendment' – Leverage, lawfare and the destruction of parliamentary democracy

At a philosophical and principled level, the Aboriginal and Torres Strait Islander Voice is illiberal, divisive and inequitable. It creates permanent race-based privilege and turns Australia into a constitutionally endorsed two-tier society. Now that the Prime Minister has revealed the words proposed to be inserted into the Constitution to establish the Voice – which I will call the 'Albanese Amendment' – it is increasingly certain that the Voice will also be a disaster as a matter of practical politics and governance.

The Voice will create constant opportunities for a tiny minority of activists to hold parliament and executive government to ransom by using the immense leverage and opportunities for lawfare carefully woven into the Albanese Amendment. It is no exaggeration to say it will cause the end of parliamentary democracy as we have known it.

That conclusion is inevitable when we analyse with care the exact words of the Albanese Amendment and the implications of those words. It is a matter of great concern that this work was not done by the Prime Minister before announcing the amendment and that since then this analysis has not been done by the Attorney-General or any of the agencies of the federal government, nor by opposition legal affairs spokesman Julian Leeser or the Coalition, nor by any of our great law firms or by any prominent KCs. The silence from our constitutional law academics, too, on critical constitutional matters arising from the Albanese Amendment is glaring.

If any of these people have done this analysis, they haven't made it public. It is a shocking failing of our public life that all these individuals and groups appear to be so busy cheering on the Albanese Amendment that they haven't bothered to scrutinise it properly. Given this determined silence on important constitutional matters, I have embarked on this job by speaking with several prominent silks and other lawyers. I am hopeful that others will follow. We should not sleepwalk into what I believe will be Australia's worst constitutional disaster in a practical sense, without proper analysis and debate. Drinking the Kool-Aid is irresponsible.

The most important sentence of the Albanese Amendment

As Tony Abbott has already outlined in his chapter, the Albanese Amendment consists of the following three sentences to be inserted into the Constitution:

- There shall be a body, to be called the Aboriginal and Torres Strait Islander Voice.

- The Aboriginal and Torres Strait Islander Voice may make representations to parliament and the executive government on matters relating to Aboriginal and Torres Strait Islander peoples.

- The parliament shall, subject to this Constitution, have power to make laws with respect to the composition, functions, powers and procedures of the Aboriginal and Torres Strait Islander Voice.

Of these sentences, the second is easily the most important. It sets out the purpose and functions of the Voice, and controls the scope of the legislative powers conferred on parliament by the third sentence. The words "subject to this Constitution" contained in the third sentence, as well as the general principles of statutory interpretation, mean that the second sentence controls and limits the meaning of the third. This may seem technical but it is critical because it means the High Court, not parliament, will be the ultimate decision-maker on the key functions, powers and procedures of the Voice.

A High Court role is assured

Legal experts warn that if parliament attempts to pass laws that limit the matters on which the Voice has to be consulted – or the process of, or timetable for, consultation – and the High Court decides these laws interfere with or hinder the scope of the Voice's essential features as set out in the second sentence of the Albanese Amendment, the High Court will simply declare the relevant laws invalid. Therefore, it is likely, for example, that any attempt by parliament to legislate that matters such as banking regulation, foreign affairs, defence or other matters were beyond the Voice's remit, or to insert exceptions for less significant or urgent matters, could be invalid.

The High Court will be able to draw implications about the Voice

Some of the country's most senior silks have told me the wording of the second sentence in the Albanese Amendment has been carefully designed to enable the High Court to find a series of far-reaching and surprising implications that the court may think necessary to give effect to the Voice, or that are reasonably incidental to its operation. In fact, in other cases the court has relied on far less to find remarkably wide implications in the Constitution. In the *Love* case, a majority of High Court judges found "metaphysical bonds" and a "deeper truth" were enough to dream up implications.

They say the court could find, for example, that the second sentence carried with it implications that the Voice be allowed reasonable time, resources, personnel, premises and budget as determined by the court to make informed representations. The court might find the second sentence could require public hearings, the right to access government papers, the right to interrogate ministers or public servants or other measures to enable the Voice to fully inform itself so it could make meaningful representations. Not only could the process of the Voice informing itself and making representations be time consuming, but the process might have to be restarted if amendments were made to a government proposal or executive action after the Voice had reviewed it.

Importantly, once the High Court finds implications about the operation of the Voice, those implications are permanent fixtures in the Constitution. Parliament has no power to alter or limit them with subsequent laws.

Equally important, if parliament passes a law (whether under the third sentence of the amendment or another head of power) or if executive government does an act without complying with the process laid down by the High Court, that law or act will be invalid.

The High Court will determine how parliament and the executive will have to respond to the Voice's representations

Relying on further implications, the High Court might find that parliament and the executive government must give bona fide and careful consideration to any representations made by the Voice and not ignore them on irrelevant or improper grounds.

Senior silks have told me that the word 'Voice' is deliberate. It gives rise to a "right to be heard" – a familiar plank of administrative law. A large body of law in the migration area, for example, says that "representations" must receive "active intellectual consideration".

It is very likely the High Court will be asked to rule that similar principles are implied in relation to the Voice, and that parliament will be required to demonstrate, perhaps by written reasons, compliance with those requirements.

The High Court could easily find such implications were necessary to give proper effect to the purpose of the Voice as set out in the second sentence of the Albanese Amendment.

The practical significance of all this is that it creates massive opportunities for litigation and lawfare. Any suggestion the deliberations or powers of the Voice will be non-justiciable – meaning beyond the courts – is, at minimum, manifestly incorrect. At worst, this suggestion is deceptive. Activists who are members of the Voice will have leverage over parliament that previously they, and we, never imagined possible.

On what matters does the Voice need to be consulted?

We were initially told we would be asked to approve a Voice to parliament and that its function would be to comment on draft legislation. The reality exposed by the Albanese Amendment is dramatically different. The Voice is to make representations on "matters", not proposed legislation.

The meaning of "matters" takes its colour from the fact the Voice can make representations not merely to parliament but to executive government. In other words, the Voice will have power to make representations not merely about proposed legislation but about any act or omission of the parliament, or the government, or any of its agencies.

So, for example, bureaucratic practices or procedures, or any changes to them, will have to be the subject of consultations with the Voice. To illustrate, if the government cuts the budget or resources available to departments dealing with Indigenous affairs, or seeks to move departmental offices from, say, Alice Springs to Darwin, it will first need to consult with the Voice and give it a chance to make representations.

Of course, the government could take the chance of not seeking representations, but this creates another opportunity for High Court lawfare and creates more leverage for activists.

Note that the word "matters" in the second sentence of the Albanese Amendment is not limited by any qualifier; for example, that the matters be "significant". On the face it, the Voice will have to be consulted even on trivial matters.

At this point we should ask what is covered by the words "relating to Aboriginal and Torres Strait Islander peoples" since this phrase is the only limit on the word "matters". Logically almost any matter can relate to Aboriginal and Torres Strait Islander peoples, in the sense that it can affect Aborigines and Torres Strait Islanders in a different manner or to a different extent to the way non-Indigenous people are affected.

The safest assumption, then, is almost any matter can relate to

Aboriginal and Torres Strait Islander peoples. In any case, the reach of the Voice will be exclusively decided not by parliament but by the High Court. More lawfare, more leverage.

Given this, we are entitled to ask: Who will be running the government? To his credit, Malcolm Turnbull was both brave and correct to get to the heart of this fundamental governance change: the Voice is looking remarkably like a third chamber of parliament.

When and how does the Voice make its representations?

We can expect parliament to make laws under the third sentence of the Albanese Amendment to set out the processes for getting the Voice involved, how and when it acts, how long it gets and what resources it is given to enable it to act. However, as explained above, parliament is not the ultimate decision-maker on these matters, meaning it is a lottery, and governments may cave in to threats of strategic litigation to avoid uncertainty and delay. Once again, more lawfare and leverage.

Moreover, while the processes and timetables for consultation with the Voice on proposed legislation should be relatively predictable, although drawn out, there may need to be fresh consultations if amendments are suggested after the Voice reviewed initial drafts of legislation.

The processes and timetables for consultation on acts or omissions by executive government that relate to Aboriginal and Torres Strait Islander peoples are likely to be more difficult to legislate with any precision, and are therefore replete with opportunities for lawfare.

While it may be safest for government to consult well in advance of any act or omission of executive government relating to Aborigines or Torres Strait Islanders, what happens if something has to be done urgently? For example, what if, due to some disease outbreak in the Northern Territory, it is necessary to undertake some urgent public health actions that in practice burden Indigenous people more than non-Indigenous people but for which there is not time, or even the information, for detailed consultation with the Voice? If the action is undertaken without adequate consultation, and the High Court will be the judge of adequacy here, the action may be invalid and have to be reversed. Another lottery, more lawfare, more leverage.

What are "representations"?

Again, the parliament will no doubt try to prescribe the form of representations in legislation passed pursuant to the third sentence of the Albanese Amendment. Again, the High Court no doubt will be asked to confirm that it agrees that the legislation adequately gives life to the constitutional demand that the Voice have the opportunity to make representations.

Issues will include whether representations can be conditional or contingent on certain events, whether the Voice has to speak unanimously or by majority (and if by majority, what majority), and whether representations have to be formal or can be informal. This should keep lawyers busy, and happy, for a while. And slow down the work of parliament and executive government.

Consequences of failure to comply with express or implied rights and powers of the Voice or duties and obligations of parliament/government

Legislation passed, or actions taken by the executive government without proper compliance with the second sentence of the Albanese Amendment as elaborated by the High Court will be invalid. The draconian consequence of invalidity will mean parliament and the executive government will live on a knife edge, constantly beholden to the Voice. It will be no exaggeration to say that all of Australian political life will have to be conducted with one eye on the Voice. The power, influence and opportunity thus handed to a small proportion of Australians will be remarkable. Parliamentary democracy as we have known it will be dead.

PART 2

EXPLAINER: The Voice in action

It is 2029. Australia is in the grip of a credit and banking crisis eerily similar to the Global Financial Crisis in 2008, caused by banks indulging in imprudent subprime lending. Unable to borrow in global markets, Australian banks are facing a liquidity crisis. Bank runs have started, and long queues of desperate depositors are starting to form outside bank branches.

The banks reach a rescue deal with the federal government. The government will provide deposit guarantees and equity capital but in return, the banks must agree to stringent new restrictions on lending. These include minimum 20 per cent deposit requirements for new housing and unsecured lending, and tough new income requirements for all loan applicants.

Urgent legislation to give effect to all this is drawn up and is about to be debated by the House of Representatives when Gunditjmara woman Cleophas Thorpe goes to the High Court seeking an injunction to stop the house from considering the legislation.

Thorpe is the leader of the Aboriginal and Torres Strait Islander Voice established in 2023 by authority of the constitutional amendments announced by Prime Minister Anthony Albanese at Garma in mid-2022. The novel body, entrenched in the Constitution, has already broken into factions and Thorpe's faction is the strongest.

Thorpe claims that the legislation cannot be introduced into the house until the Voice has had a chance to consider it fully and make detailed representations. She says the legislation affects Aboriginal and Torres Strait Islanders very differently from non-Indigenous Australians because of their relative poverty. She says that the legislation raises serious issues of indirect discrimination and requires careful analysis to see if its effect on Indigenous peoples can be reduced. Thorpe argues that Aboriginal and Torres Strait Islanders should, at minimum, be largely exempt from the 20 per cent deposit requirement and the borrower income requirements.

The government points to provisions in the legislation establishing the Voice passed under the new constitutional amendment which say banking regulation is not a matter for the Voice and which also say that the Voice can be bypassed in emergencies.

The High Court disagrees. It holds that parliament has no power to prescribe matters allegedly beyond the reach of the Voice. It points out that it alone has power to decide if legislation "relates to Aboriginal and Torres Strait Islander" people (to quote Albanese's wording that was agreed to at a referendum).

The court says that legislation which purports to exclude the Voice from considering matters which the High Court thinks "relate to" Aboriginal and Torres Strait Islander people is invalid.

The High Court goes further and says that the attempt to bypass the Voice in emergencies is clearly invalid. Albanese's constitutional amendment contained no exemption for emergencies or any temporal or other limits on the Voice's power to scrutinise legislation in advance.

Indeed, the High Court says that to give proper effect to the constitutional requirement that the Voice has the opportunity to make representations to parliament on proposed legislation, one must imply that the Voice be given reasonable notice of intended legislation and the time and resources to consider it properly.

Once that is done, there is an implied obligation on parliament to give reasonable consideration to the representations made by the Voice and give reasons if it rejects those representations. Legislation that does not meet these requirements will be invalid, says the High Court.

Although it does not necessarily agree with Thorpe's arguments about the need for specific exemptions for Indigenous people from the proposed law, the court does agree that the proposed legislation "relates to" Aboriginal and Torres Strait Islanders because it affects them differently to non-Indigenous people and therefore should have been given to the Voice in time for it to make representations to the parliament before submission to the House of Representatives.

The High Court says that a reasonable time for the Voice to consider the legislation in its final agreed form is at least a month before submission to the house. If there are material amendments made to the legislation after the Voice has finished with it but before passage, the amended legislation must go back to the Voice for a further month-long consultation.

The government is shocked. The High Court heard Thorpe's application urgently, but still, in that time, several regional banks have become insolvent. Pointing to the increasing panic among depositors queuing up to get their money back, and looming insolvency among even the major banks, the government begs Thorpe to convene the Voice urgently and finalise consultations within days. Thorpe hates the banks and couldn't care less about depositors who come from coloniser stock. She is not inclined to agree to the government's request. Unless of course her separate wish list is satisfied. That list contains radical demands that, in 2023, many Australians would have thought would not form part of the Voice. But Thorpe says her radical demands are a small price to pay to save the banking system.

PART 3

The Voice debate is shallow by design

Returning to 2022, it beggars belief that the federal Attorney-General and the Prime Minister have not released legal advice they must have surely sought and received about the constitutional implications of entrenching a race-based Voice in our founding document. That legal advice ought to be ours given that the government wants voters to alter how we are governed. If Mark Dreyfus and Anthony Albanese have not sought and received legal advice, that is a damning dereliction of their duty to treat the Constitution with care.

It beggars belief that the shadow Attorney-General has not done this work either. Or, if he has, why he is not asking laser-sharp questions about the constitutional implications of the Voice.

It beggars belief that our most esteemed constitutional law professors have spent more time firing off one-liners and insults than the harder, more sober work of analysing the possibility of the High Court's role after plonking a new body into the Constitution.

After all, in a logical world, when a group of people recommends an idea, claiming it is a reform that will improve our society, they would explain it to us. Most reforms, after all, involve a group of winners and a group of losers. Economists call it concentrated benefits, when the upside is shared by a small group, and diffuse costs meaning the downside is spread across a larger one.

When you want to put that idea in our Constitution, working out the details, thrashing out the cost-benefit arguments, so we can intelligently decide whether to vote yes or no, is even more important. Alas, those proposing this change think little of logic, and less of voters.

The result is a debate that is both shallow and confused. Sadly, that appears to be by design. In some respects, it is a symbol of Australian intellectual life in the 21st century where so many groups comprised of very smart people are either derelict about seeking the details of an idea that is claimed to be a reform, or they are hiding those details from us.

It has been dismal to watch so many successful people - lawyers, academics, business men and women, politicians, and hordes in the media - suspend intellectual faculties that they would normally use to full effect in their daily lives. Business leaders have signed on to a constitutional change with no regard for their duties to shareholders. Few politicians, and even lawyers, have sought expert legal advice about the constitutional implications of the transfer of power from parliament and executive government to the Voice. Whole swathes of the media have joined the bandwagon to the point where the ABC will routinely reflect a chorus line of 'yes, yes, yes' chanting to the Voice, akin to *that* scene in the movie, *When Harry Met Sally*.

By joining the movement early, not asking questions then, many of these people are now so invested they refuse to think rationally about important principles being undermined by the Voice and the very real dangers of this new body. Their desperation to attach their name to a moment in history, to be mentioned in dispatches, even a footnote, without considering the future implications of the Voice is sign of how anti-intellectual this public debate has become.

We are being asked to vote yes on the basis of 'she'll be right, mate." The 'yes' case is not just shallow. It is confused, to use a neutral term. For example, legal academics Greg Craven and George Williams have advocated for the Voice on the basis that it is a "modest" change which achieves large reconciliation benefits in return for minimal change to our democratic procedures. The Prime Minister has said it is simply a matter of good manners. However, while our academic friends mean well, it reeks of arrogance or delusion to suggest that the High Court will not have a major role in shaping the Voice, given the proposed powers in the Constitution. I am not a reckless gambler willing to take Craven's word that the High Court won't be involved in interpreting a constitutionally entrenched Voice. How can he possibly presume to know this?

I'd rather take the word of Australia's leading silks who actually argue constitutional cases before the High Court. Though insultingly dismissed by advocates as fear mongers and Chicken Littles, these careful, practical silks have painstakingly laid out for me, and thus for readers, the reasons why the proposed amendment will give the Voice startling power, leverage and influence.

Moreover, academic views about the modesty of the proposed change, are not even shared by their more worldly fellow advocates.

In mid-August, the co-chair of Australians for Indigenous Constitutional Recognition Danny Gilbert was quoted as saying the "whole point" of a Voice to Parliament would be for it to be influential and politically powerful. "And why shouldn't it be so?" Thank you, Mr Gilbert, for clarifying that much.

Let's recall what Malcolm Turnbull said of this power shift in 2017: "Every single law that goes through the parliament, whether it is tax, whether it is defence, whether it is social security, whether it is health - they all affect Aboriginal and Torres Strait Islander people because they're part of the Australian community. And that would mean that that assembly would have the right, if it chose, to examine every piece of legislation. It would be, in effect, a third chamber. I don't think it's a good idea and if it were put up in a referendum, it would go down in flames. That's my view."

Though Turnbull now supports a race-based Voice in the Constitution, he recognizes this will be a major change to our current constitutional arrangements: "I have reservations about it, I have misgivings and it will be an enormous change to the way our parliamentary system works. I still believe it will make a very big change. It's not a symbolic change, it is not like the republic, which was largely symbolic. This is conferring real power, real political power, to the Voice," Turnbull told the ABC's 7.30 *Report* in mid-August 2022.

Indeed, there is more than a little arrogance in demanding that we bet the stability of our current constitutional arrangements on the pious hopes of academics who trade in insults and quips when Malcolm Turnbull and a bevy of silks are telling us the Albanese Amendment is a very major change.

The Voice is, at heart, a transfer of power. And power isn't created out of thin air. By putting it in the Constitution in the format of the three sentences that comprise the Albanese Amendment, the power comes from somewhere – namely it shifts power from parliament and executive government to a race-based constitutionally entrenched body. And the timing of that power shift is critical: it is meant to happen before the next two parts of the Uluru Statement, the truth telling and treaty parts, are pursued.

Admittedly, the poor quality of the debate is not helped by the public silence among legal experts who understand the dangers that could very likely arise from entrenching the Voice in the Constitution. Unlike academics, these senior lawyers, most of them KCs, work in the real world, arguing real cases before real courts. Their silence points to another key feature disfiguring this debate, namely the attempt to bully, coerce and silence opponents.

Put simply, the public silence of these lawyers and KCs is a case of self-protection. They are not willing to become political cannon fodder over this referendum proposal. It is a damning indictment, not of them, but of our public discourse that constitutional lawyers whose expertise was gained from actual cases in the High Court, rather than sat university, are not willing to publicly raise their concerns or offer their advice for fear of having their careers damaged by the zeitgeist. It means we only hear from lawyers who are part of that zeitgeist.

One KC told me if any lawyer raised legal concerns Voice activists "would go to town on us. There'll be an outcry for weeks. You just get hammered."

"Law firms would say 'we can't brief him because he's been branded as an extremist.' You would have judges treat you as an extremist. You would be marginalized and ostracized on your own [barristers'] floor and within the profession," says one KC. "When a client googles a barrister and if this stuff comes up, they will say "no, no, he's too hot. We want Mr. Nice. They don't want to send in someone seen as public enemy number one," he adds.

It will also harm chances of promotion to the bench: "You will even be isolated, discredited within the coalition. Because if they're talking about appointing somebody, they don't want someone who's a lightning rod. They'll say, 'no, not him. We just don't want to have that row at the moment.'"

When the ABC's Sarah Ferguson says only those voting 'yes' are "on the right side of history" the tactics are clear. It is to malign those who have concerns about the Voice, how it will work in practice.

It is troubling when our most esteemed KCs feel unable to offer their expertise to publicly discuss concerns about the transfer of power from the parliament and the executive to a race-based Voice and about the role of the High Court in this transfer of power. But you can't blame them. When Craven damned them as Chicken Littles and terrorizing fearmongers, it proved that they were right to stay silent. Unlike academics, these silks don't have tenure.

However, this points to a hollowed out and debased public debate, if we can even use that word, where emotion and slogans trump reasoned analysis. We have become a society that celebrates our own dumbing down.

If the Voice turns out to be a rolled gold disaster, and a permanently entrenched one, we will all ask ourselves: how did we let this happen? If we were carried away with the emotion and the goodwill – the "vibe of the thing" – and failed to insist on the details, we will all deserve the contempt of our children.

Moreover, a major constitutional change pushed through with the help of bullying, coercion, obfuscation and silencing will be no basis for reconciliation. It will, sadly, be the opposite.

4

CONSTITUTIONAL CHANGE BY STEALTH

Chris Merritt

When Anthony Albanese addressed the Garma festival on 30 July 2022, he provided a preliminary outline of his proposed change to the Australian Constitution that would create an Indigenous Voice to parliament. The new provision, which he described as a starting point, would consist of three sentences establishing an institution whose structure, jurisdiction and powers are uncertain. Because the prime minister's three sentences are silent on those issues, they will need to be determined later by others - not by the voting public.

At this referendum, the community is being treated with disdain. We are being asked to endorse a new constitutional entity while having only a limited idea of what we are voting for. That means the community cannot make a fully informed choice. Any entity that is established in such circumstances will be a weak addition to the Australian polity, forever vulnerable to the charge that it lacks democratic legitimacy because key details were withheld.

The referendum on the Voice should be rejected because it is an attempt to change the constitution by stealth.

Seven years ago, when constitutional recognition of this country's Indigenous people was again on the national agenda, I was among those arguing for change. But this particular proposal is unworthy of support. Key elements of the proposed institution have either been kept secret or are simply unknown. The few details that have been made public make it clear that core parts of the scheme favoured by the Indigenous community will not be part of the scheme that is on offer.

The government says it will determine detailed plans for the Voice after the referendum. That will give politicians more say on this constitutional entity than the voting public. But key aspects of the new institution will also be determined by the High Court in order to clarify issues that have been left unresolved in the provision unveiled at the Garma festival.

The Constitution derives its legitimacy from the people of this country - not from judges and politicians. It is therefore regrettable that all the details of a new constitutional entity will not be submitted to the people for approval or rejection. Few would buy a house sight unseen. So why would we change the Constitution before knowing exactly what the change will mean?

Once the three sentences from Garma are part of the Constitution, the involvement of the High Court is inevitable. The Constitution means what the High Court says it means. And because the meaning of those three sentences is not entirely clear, the court will have a major say on the future of the Voice.

This is undesirable for two reasons: the first is that it would embroil the court in debates that are, in essence, political. The second reason concerns the court's recent propensity for judicial creativity on the subject of Indigenous affairs. In a 2020 case known as *Love* and *Thoms*, the High Court punched a hole in the doctrine of equality before the law in order to prevent foreign criminals with Aboriginal ancestry from being deported. One judge even invoked the metaphysical while inventing a constitutional restriction on the government's power to deport foreign criminals. If there is one subject that is best resolved elsewhere, it is the future of the Voice.

Avoiding difficult issues instead of confronting them in open debate might be viewed by some as a clever tactic to secure a political win. But this is the Constitution. If a change is made, it will be with us forever - either uniting or dividing the nation. Preventing voters from making a fully informed decision on the Voice does nothing to persuade the community to accept the proposed institution. If the referendum succeeds in these circumstances, those on the losing side could argue that the Voice had been secured by deception - poisoning community relations and bringing the new institution into disrepute. This is the reverse of the outcome that those of goodwill who support the Voice are seeking to achieve. It would be a disservice to those in the Indigenous community who, unlike the government, have been open and transparent about the sort of institution they would like to see entrenched in the Constitution.

The proposed constitutional provision that was outlined at the Garma festival fails to meet the expectations of those seeking to entrench in the Constitution a representative body exclusively for Indigenous Australians that must be consulted by parliament.

The word "representative" does not appear in the three sentences Albanese wants to add to the Constitution, nor do they contain any suggestion that parliament would be obliged to consult the new body. That means any legislation enacted by Labor after the referendum to address those issues could be repealed by subsequent parliaments - effectively destroying the Voice as a representative body but leaving a shell of the organisation due to the limited nature of the proposed constitutional entrenchment. Is this what Voice advocates want?

The provision outlined by the prime minister is so lacking in detail that a future government could enact a law giving itself the authority to appoint anyone to the proposed body, regardless of ethnic background, and charge them with speaking on behalf of Indigenous people. Why would supporters of the Voice consider this to be an improvement?

If the three sentences from the Garma festival are endorsed at the referendum, it would give Labor a hollow victory, secured by gamesmanship - not a full and frank debate within the community about the structure, power and jurisdiction of the new constitutional entity. The government, it seems, wants that debate to be dominated by politicians once the voting it over.

Albanese's speech at the Garma festival, as opposed to the terms of the proposed constitutional change, placed emphasis on "consulting" Indigenous people. "It's about consulting Aboriginal and Torres Strait Islander peoples on the decisions that affect you," said Albanese. "Nothing more – but nothing less."

But if consulting the Voice is so important, why is there no reference to this in the three sentences that would form part of the Constitution? Instead of imposing such a constitutional requirement on parliament, the new provision would give the Voice permission to make representations to parliament and the government. This is anodyne. Such a right is already enjoyed by every citizen and community group, regardless of ethnic background or constitutional standing. This what the three sentences say:

1. There shall be a body, to be called the Aboriginal and Torres Strait Islander Voice.

2. The Aboriginal and Torres Strait Islander Voice may make representations to Parliament and the Executive Government on matters relating to Aboriginal and Torres Strait Islander People.

3. The Parliament shall, subject to this Constitution, have power to make laws with respect to the composition, functions, powers and procedures of the Aboriginal and Torres Strait Islander Voice.

The significance of these three sentences is to be found not just in what they say, but in what they do not say. The second sentence does not clearly define and thereby limit the role of the institution. The language is permissive - the Voice "may make representations". But it does not restrict the Voice to the sole function of making representations. If there had been an intention to limit its role in this way the second sentence would have included one more word making it clear that the Voice "may *only* make representations" on matters that relate to Aboriginal and Torres Strait Islander people.

The absence of such a clear limit on its role leaves the way open for additional functions and powers to be given to this body. This is consistent with the fact that the final sentence of the proposed constitutional provision gives parliament the power to make laws about the powers of the Voice. If it were to have only the one function of providing representations, the second sentence gives the Voice all the authority it needs. There would be no need for the reference in the third sentence which gives parliament authority to make laws about the powers of the Voice. The intention - unexpressed by the government - is clearly to vest this body with additional powers once the referendum is out of the way. What those powers might be is unknown.

The uncertainty does not end there. What, exactly, are "matters relating to" Aboriginal and Torres Strait Islander People? If the government had intended to confine the role of the Voice to Indigenous affairs, it could have restricted the body to providing representations on matters that arise under section 51(xxvi) of the Constitution. That was not done. Section 51(xxvi), commonly known as the race power, reads: *The Parliament shall, subject to this Constitution, have power to make laws for the peace, order, and good government of the Commonwealth with respect to...the people of any race for whom it is deemed necessary to make special laws.*

This section is the constitutional head of power that gives the federal government authority to make laws for Indigenous people when it is deemed necessary to make such special laws. By declining to use section 51(xxvi) to define and limit the reach of the Voice, the proposed wording again suggests that the way is open for arguments, once the Voice is established, about whether it can legitimately involve itself in matters that go beyond Indigenous affairs.

Unless the boundaries on the role of the Voice are more clearly defined, there is the prospect of High Court test cases in which the court, not the voting public, would be asked to decide how far the Voice should involve itself in matters that extend beyond Indigenous affairs.

Remarks by Indigenous Affairs minister, Linda Burney, on 26 September 2022 sought to address this concern – but they serve only to strengthen my concern about the subjects on which the voice might eventually seek to involve itself.

Burney stated in *The Australian* newspaper that the Voice would advise the government on matters that were of "direct relevance" to Aboriginal people and would have a "direct effect" on them. She said this would include matters like land rights, native title, cultural water allocations and housing. It would not include defence and taxation.

But how much weight can be placed on this assurance? If that is really the government's intention, why didn't it include these limits on the role of the Voice in the provision that would be inserted into the Constitution? In the same interview, the minister appeared to undermine the force of her own statements by conceding that the role of the Voice would be determined not by her, but by a vote in parliament:

> What seems to be lost on everyone is that at the end of the day it will be the parliament that will determine the shape and the role of the Voice. It's up to how parliament wants to use the advisory body and what the advisory body feels is appropriate. It's not up to me to say 'This is what it will be'.

So, despite the assurances from the minister, she has confirmed that politicians will determine the shape and role of the Voice. Right now, there is no model for the Voice and no detail about its exact jurisdiction, powers and makeup. We are being asked for a blank cheque so details can be filled in after the referendum by Labor and the High Court. In order to be accepted as legitimate, these details need to be made public before the referendum. If they are withheld, only to be determined later, there is a clear risk to the future standing of the resulting institution.

Other parts of the Constitution are the result of exhaustive debates that took place at a series of constitutional conventions in the 1890s. People knew what they were voting for when they approved the Constitution. That will not be the case with the Voice.

If the referendum succeeds, Burney's statements will not be conclusive. The High Court will inevitably be asked to decide if the form of words used in Albanese's second sentence - "matters relating to" - should be given an expansive or restrictive meaning. Regardless of what parliament might say about the reach of the Voice in any subsequent legislation, the High Court will determine if this entity can involve itself in the formation of laws and policies that affect the entire community. If those three sentences are approved, the High Court will have the exclusive right to determine what "matters relating to" means. Parliament will be powerless to intervene.

The history of this particular aspect of the Voice might provide an insight into the possible reasons why the government's proposal, with its relatively vague limits on the role of the new institution, leaves the way open for test cases that could extend its jurisdiction. For the government to impose clear boundaries on the Voice before the referendum, no matter how wide those boundaries might be, would have meant rejecting the views of leading proponents of the Voice.

In July 2021, the final report to the federal government on the Indigenous Voice Co-Design Process considered what limits should be placed on the subjects that would warrant advice from the Voice. That report shows the national co-design group considered and rejected limiting its involvement to matters that invoked section 51(xxvi), matters that concerned laws and policies specifically directed to Aborigines and Torres Strait Islanders, and matters referred to the Voice by the federal government. Instead, that report says "all these more restrictive approaches were rejected". The national co-design group wanted no limits on the subjects in which the Voice could become involved, and stated in the report:

> Under the final proposal, advice would be provided on the laws and policies that the National Voice sees as of greatest importance to Aboriginal and Torres Strait Islander peoples. Restricting the scope of the advice function would diminish the role of the National Voice as a national, broad-based representative body for all Aboriginal and Torres Strait Islander people and reduce its ability to influence the Australian Parliament and Government.

> Aboriginal and Torres Strait Islander peoples have their own specific priorities, in addition to the same concerns as non-Indigenous Australians, and the role of a National Voice would be to reflect those priorities in providing its advice. Aboriginal and Torres Strait Islander peoples are affected by a broad range of laws and policies, both those directed specifically at Aboriginal and Torres Strait Islander peoples and those for all Australians.

By choosing relatively vague words to define the boundaries of the new institution's involvement in public affairs, the government might have lessened the impact of its clear rejection of the push for a constitutionally entrenched representative body for Indigenous people. Entrenching the representative nature of the Voice in the Constitution was favoured in 2017's final report of the Referendum Council. The council's first recommendation says:

> That a referendum be held to provide in the Australian Constitution for a representative body that gives Aboriginal and Torres Strait Islander First Nations a Voice to the Commonwealth Parliament.

The three sentences from the Garma festival also indicate that the government has rejected the option of entrenching a constitutional obligation for parliament to consult the Voice. But Albanese's speech at the same event strongly endorsed the need for consultation. So, until the prime minister addresses this issue, there must be a possibility that this proposal will reappear in statutory form. To abandon it entirely, and replace it with a constitutionalised system of mere representations by the Voice, would mark a clear break with the Indigenous community's wishes. It would mean Labor has decided to walk away from the position outlined in the Final Report of the Indigenous Voice Co-Design Process. That report outlines a cascading series of obligations for parliament and the government to consult the Voice on some matters and then an "expectation" that they would consult the Voice on other matters. It says:

> Parliament and Government would have an obligation to consult on primary legislation that either overwhelmingly relates to Aboriginal and Torres Strait Islander peoples; or is a special measure for Aboriginal and Torres Strait Islander people within the definition of the Racial Discrimination Act 1975 (Cth).

Albanese needs to explain whether the obligation for parliament to consult the Voice and the proposal for the Voice to represent

Indigenous people are both dead or whether they have simply been removed from the referendum proposal and will reappear as part of the legislative scheme that will be required to give form to the Voice. If those elements of the Voice are to reappear after the referendum - which seems likely - they will not be entrenched in the Constitution and could be changed by future parliaments.

Those who will vote at the referendum, including supporters of the Voice, would be better informed if they knew in advance whether the obligation to consult this body will be imposed on parliament and whether this obligation will also extend to the formation of government policy - as favoured by the final report of the Indigenous Voice Co-Design Process. The community might also benefit from knowing whether the government plans to give the Voice a role at international forums, as proposed by that final report, and how it would deal with conflicting views within the Voice.

The lack of clarity in the three sentences from Garma amounts to an invitation to litigate - if they are entrenched in the Constitution. The High Court - with its dubious recent history on Indigenous affairs - would come under pressure to give meaning to the new provision. This will do nothing to address the concerns of those who fear the Voice referendum could open the door to an erosion of democratic legitimacy. Once a new provision is inserted in the Constitution it cannot be changed by parliament. The greater the uncertainty about the meaning of Albanese's three sentences, the greater the transfer of power to the High Court. And given the court's record, this is something that should be avoided.

The clearest warning about what could go wrong can be seen in the history of section 92 of the Constitution which, thanks to judicial interpretation, no longer means what the plain words say. This provision, which was fundamental to federation, is supposed to guarantee that "trade commerce and intercourse among the states . . . shall be absolutely free". Instead, successive High Courts have interpreted this to mean they will only strike down barriers between the states if they do not pass a test, created by the court, known as "structured proportionality". This is difficult to reconcile with the clear intention of those who drafted the Constitution that there should be no impediment to freedom of movement from one end of this continent to the other.

The government's drafting of the proposed constitutional provision for the Voice is flawed - perhaps intentionally so. It leaves the way open for advocacy groups to run test cases that could change the Voice in ways that might surprise those who will vote at the referendum. It happened with section 92, so unless the three sentences from Garma are clarified before the referendum, there is a risk it could happen with the Voice.

The intention of those who argue for constitutional entrenchment is that the Voice will be a benign addition to the nation's founding document that will unite rather than divide this country. That goal, however, is sharply at odds with the patronising manner in which the community is being denied the information it needs in order to be fully informed. If the government remains reluctant to share the details about how this entity would work, its gamesmanship should not be rewarded. The only safe course would be to vote 'no'.

Suggested reading

Indigenous Voice Co-design Process Final Report to the Australian Government, (Commonwealth of Australia, 2021).

5

WHAT CONSERVATIVE VOICE SUPPORTERS GET WRONG ABOUT CONSTITUTIONAL RECOGNITION

Bernard Samuelson

Heartfelt but not hard-headed

The movement to recognise Indigenous Australians in the Constitution is adopting the only method which has any hope of persuading the electorate to support constitutional change. This is strategically astute. Altering Australia's constitution is a very difficult task and because of this, Indigenous leaders, such as Noel Pearson, are seeking bipartisan support to establish what Pearson refers to as "common ground with the right." Hence, the recruitment of conservative writers, thinkers, lawyers, churchmen, and politicians to support the Indigenous recognition model endorsed in the Uluru Statement From the Heart (see page ix). This model proposes to enshrine an Indigenous 'Voice to Parliament' in the Constitution.

Notable conservative figures – who include Liberal Party parliamentarians, venerable 'black letter' jurists, leaders from the business sector, law firms, and investment banks, as well as Christian prelates from across the denominational divide – have all declared their support for the Voice. The model for which they advocate would formally require parliament to hear the views of Indigenous peoples, as presented by a properly-constituted consultative, representative body, when laws and policies affecting Indigenous interests are being made.

Conservative Voice supporters have been part of the historic shift in sentiment regarding Indigenous affairs. This shift in national consciousness is due, in part, to current generations having greater knowledge of European settlement of the Australian continent and its consequences. Awareness of, and guilt about, the destruction of Aboriginal society after 1788 has evoked a sense of national shame over the long Indigenous experience of racism, domination, marginalization, and alienation in their own land. This has built support for a process of 'Reconciliation' to help overcome the social, economic, and other disadvantages that some Indigenous people suffer today.

These are the heartfelt sentiments that prompt conservatives to endorse constitutional recognition in pursuit of a reconciled nation. "Can we tolerate a nation where Indigenous people can feel estranged?" asks the tough-minded conservative commentator and whole-hearted advocate, Chris Kenny. "If our institutions, our foundational document, can belatedly embrace Indigenous Australians, would it not benefit us all? Would it not make our country bigger? Would it not complete our nation?"

The conservative case in support of the Voice expresses a heartfelt desire to pay a kind of national penance for the original sins of Australian colonisation; to avoid repeating the mistakes of the past; and to make right the suffering of Indigenous people during the European history of Australia. The thinking is that an amended set of constitutional rules governing the relationship between Indigenous and non-Indigenous Australia will give Indigenous Australians a constitutional guarantee of fairer treatment. Whereas Indigenous Australians have been mistreated by governments prejudiced and hostile to their best interests, the

Voice will give them a rightful say in all aspects of governance affecting Indigenous people.

The idea is that a formalised process of engagement with parliament will deliver far more than symbolic reconciliation by empowering Indigenous people to take control of their destiny. The Voice is thereby presented as marking a substantive change which will lead to better policies intended to address Indigenous disadvantage. As such, the Voice is both practical and aspirational.

For distinguished constitutional scholar, Greg Craven, whose conservative credentials are unquestioned, recognising Indigenous Australians in the Constitution is "a profound moral question, the response to which can only come from the heart of the Australian people as a whole"; it also "understands simultaneously the intense need for a practical solution and the reality that the payload of any true solution ultimately will be moral in character".

Bringing these threads together, conservative philosopher, Damien Freeman, argues that this is the opportunity "for a new defining moment: when the Australian nation unites to acknowledge the past and declare its aspirations for the future".

The quest for ultimate reconciliation between Indigenous and non-Indigenous Australia is grounded in what is presented as a thoroughly practical view of Australian history, seeking both to explain the present and to chart a better future. According to the view of the history of the nation's founding advanced by Freeman, "Indigenous people continue to bear the brunt of failures flowing from the defining moment in 1788 that set the course for modern Australia." This, in turn, accounts for the fact that "Indigenous people remain among the most disadvantaged people in Australia today." This is something contemporary Australians must recognize, says Freeman:

> [For] the appalling health, employment, and education statistics among Indigenous people...are consequences of more than two centuries of policy-making, all of which has its foundations in the terms on which this continent was settled.

Views such as this are significant and are not to be dismissed as mere sentimentality. For the true conservative knows that if traditional institutions are to endure, they must remain in-touch with the prevailing cultural values of society.

It may therefore be wise for conservatives to argue that Australia's constitutional arrangements must evolve in order to remain aligned with the democratically-expressed aims and aspirations of the Australian people whose interests those arrangements are intended to serve. It might follow from this that Indigenous Australians do, indeed, deserve a special place in our Constitution, affording them a status that would reflect the special place of Indigenous people in the nation's past, present, and future.

Yet if they are to remain at all relevant, modern conservatives must also be prepared to counter a cultural sentiment, no matter how heartfelt, if they believe that it could pose a social or cultural threat to Australia's institutions, and thereby to the interests of the people whom the institutions are intended to serve.

Identifying what should endure and what might need to evolve requires hard-headed scrutiny of the claims made by advocates of constitutional change. This is especially so when it is claimed that constitutional reconciliation of the nation will create a political mechanism to improve the shameful social malaise suffered by the most disadvantaged Indigenous Australians.

A realist dissent

The conservative case bends over backwards to understand the perspective of Indigenous leaders. At the same time, they seek to address the roots of the ongoing plight of disadvantaged Indigenous Australians which lie in the supposed two centuries of interconnected history and policy-making. However, this has meant conservative supporters of the Voice have had to accept the major political claim, long made by Indigenous activists, that the historical legacy of dispossession, oppression and destruction of Aboriginal society explains the present status and condition of Indigenous people in modern Australia.

This is a flawed and highly-partisan historical account and has led to a misleading interpretation of the causes of contemporary Indigenous disadvantage. Attributing Indigenous suffering to the original sins of 1788 simply endorses the major political claims that have been made by Indigenous activists since the rise of the modern Aboriginal Rights movement in the 1960s.

These claims soon became the operating assumptions which informed Indigenous policy-making. In reality, modern Australia's worst Indigenous suffering and deprivation in the dysfunctional remote 'homeland' communities has been caused by the continuing implementation by Australian governments of the policies of 'Aboriginal Self-Determination' which began in the 1970s. In effect, the conservative case is endorsing the misconceptions and flawed thinking about Indigenous affairs that have led directly to social catastrophe in remote Indigenous communities where appalling health, employment, and education statistics have been recorded.

The quest to right the wrongs of Australian history that began in the 1970s, when government support was provided to enable Indigenous people to live separately in traditional ways on their traditional lands, has made things worse for the most disadvantaged Indigenous Australians who now endure Third-world living conditions in a First-world country. Drawing so heavily, as it does, on a flawed understanding of the history of Indigenous affairs, the conservative case which is presented as a practical prescription to overcome Indigenous disadvantage is similarly and dangerously flawed.

At best, conservative supporters of the Voice are naïve about Aboriginal politics and about the aims and interests of the Indigenous political class whose primary objective is to create a political structure that will help sustain in perpetuity the 'separatist' homeland experiment. Therefore, despite detailed realist accounts of the true history of Indigenous affairs to the contrary, the heartfelt conservative case is not only based on major misconceptions that still muddle thinking about Indigenous policy; it also risks ensuring this flawed thinking about Indigenous affairs is embedded in the Constitution.

A constitutionally-enshrined Voice threatens to grant Indigenous leaders who remain committed to the failed self-determination agenda of the 1970s a privileged position from which to exert political influence over parliamentary decision-making regarding the future of remote communities. If the Voice proposal is accepted by the Australian people, conservative supporters of the Voice will be complicit in perpetuating circumstances that have led to the exclusion of the most deprived Indigenous Australians from freedoms and opportunities that other Australians take for granted.

The true history of Indigenous disadvantage

Conservative advocates for the Voice argue that it will finally hold the nation to account for historic injustices perpetrated against Indigenous peoples. Their case endorses the argument, long made by the overwhelming majority of Indigenous leaders, that entrenched Indigenous disadvantage derives from failure to address the national shame of colonial dispossession and oppression.

European Australia has a long history of prejudice and exclusion of Indigenous peoples. However, the political claim that historical forces dating from the arrival of the First Fleet remain responsible for the poverty and exclusion endured by under-privileged Indigenous people in contemporary Australia is simplistic. It also distorts the recent history of Indigenous affairs and overlooks the real causes of present-day Indigenous suffering.

In fact, the truths of Australian history were acknowledged in the 1970s since when the two principal objectives of Indigenous policy have been to account for the historical record and to make amends. In order to understand the real causes of contemporary Indigenous suffering, it is important to recall, first, the speed of the response to the rise of the Aboriginal Rights movement in the 1960s, and, second, the speed with which the historical grievances of Aboriginal activists were addressed by government.

Acknowledgement of the historical truth about Australia's founding formed the basis of the separatist policy of Aboriginal Self-Determination promoted under the Whitlam and Fraser Governments in the 1970s. This policy was based on the postcolonial rhetoric of the fledgling Aboriginal Rights movement which, by shining a light on history of invasion and settlement, demanded a full reckoning for the toll it had taken on Indigenous people.

The idea behind the policy was that advancement of Aboriginal people required separate rights and separate development on their own traditional lands. This was to take place under the guidance and direction of their own political, legal, and social organisations so as to ensure that traditional cultural and spiritual values could be restored and retained. Self-determination was intended to address the historic wrongs by allowing Aborigines to return to their 'country', to live on their traditional lands in traditional ways, and to maintain their traditional cultural and spiritual connection to ancestral homelands.

In practice, however, the policies of Aboriginal self-determination have unfolded as a continuing national tragedy in the 1200 remote homeland communities across Australia. This is the true story of contemporary Indigenous disadvantage exposed by realist accounts that first appeared in the 2000s detailing the nature and causes of the entrenched social problems that plagued many communities.

Realist accounts focused on analysing specifically how self-determination contributed directly to creating the appalling living standards found in Indigenous communities. They identified the prevalence of passive welfare dependence in the absence of economic opportunity in remote areas, the scourge of grog, drugs, and pornography, and the effects of 'humbugging', overcrowded public housing, and communal rather than private ownership of land. Realists explained how these factors had combined to break down the social norms regulating work, family, and community life in many communities — a breakdown measured by the suffering of Indigenous people, especially women and children, due to epidemic levels of communal violence, and physical and sexual abuse. Realist accounts of Indigenous policy drove home the vital truth that entrenched Indigenous disadvantage has not been the result of the nation having done too little to address the wrongs of the past.

The real issue in Indigenous affairs is not the alleged lack of national accountability for the historical causes of Indigenous disadvantage. Rather, it is that the worst outcomes experienced by Indigenous people are due to well-meaning, but misguided, policies intended to atone for historic wrongs. These policies, which have cost the nation tens of thousands of billions of dollars of public expenditure, have resulted in violence, squalor and dysfunction. Continuation of the separatist experiments in the homelands condemns those

20 per cent of Indigenous people living in remote Australia to appalling social outcomes and exclusion from the benefits and opportunities of modern Australia.

The conservative case for the Voice makes little, if any, reference to these substantive and crucial matters of Indigenous policy-making. It is silent on the impact of Aboriginal self-determination but persists in asserting that the only effective way to address Indigenous disadvantage is by addressing historic wrongs. And it is silent on what should be the central policy issues in Indigenous affairs: the future of the homeland communities, and whether governments should continue to fund services to prop up the failed social and political experiments on communally-owned Aboriginal land that have condemned generations of Indigenous Australians to abject poverty.

Hence, the conservative case is blind to the logical policy response: relocation to populated areas where there are jobs, quality schools, available services, and better opportunities for a brighter future. Naivety about Aboriginal politics also means that conservative proponents of the Voice are unaware that this is the response option that the Indigenous political class attempts to stymie by making the political path to implementation next to impossible for Australian governments.

The Aboriginal politics of the Voice

Conservative advocates of constitutional recognition insist that reform must not be merely symbolic but deliver substantive change. Even if it does not have formal power, the Voice must have a constitutionally guaranteed status and position whereby it may exercise meaningful influence over parliamentary deliberations on Indigenous policy.

As Freeman puts it (more tellingly than he admits, given the longstanding focus of Indigenous activism on sovereignty and a treaty), this would make recognition "the culmination of years of Indigenous advocacy for substantive reform of the way Indigenous policy-making happens in this country under the Constitution." According to federal Liberal MP and now shadow attorney general, Julian Leeser, the objective must be to put in place a political structure that will help to ensure "the failed policies of the past don't happen again."

This is a brave aspiration. In all areas of public policy, those interested in good outcomes should always be skeptical of political claims made by those with vested interests. The demands of the Indigenous political class are endorsed and echoed by the conservative case which is to secure "constitutional and structural reforms to transform this centuries-old dysfunctional relationship into a new functional relationship, one that enables governments to assist Indigenous communities in becoming empowered and productive". Yet this should be a red flag to those familiar with the history of Aboriginal politics.

Realist accounts of Indigenous disadvantage for a time inspired a fundamental change in the Indigenous debate earlier this century. Emphasis moved away from a focus on historical and political issues – dispossession, sovereignty, and a treaty - towards concern for the policy-led downward spiral into the social dysfunction that blights Indigenous communities.

This debate, together with recognition of the failure of Aboriginal separatism, spurred the development under the Howard Government of so-called 'Practical Reconciliation'. Its aim was to 'close the gap' in social outcomes by better integrating and elevating the conditions of all Indigenous people and communities by means of access to the benefits and opportunities available in mainstream society.

The principal innovation in Indigenous policy under the Practical Reconciliation era was to eliminate the separatist approach which had prevailed during the period when Indigenous communities gradually collapsed into chronic dysfunction. One key decision was taken by the Howard Government in 2004 to abolish the corrupt and failing peak Aboriginal-controlled administrative body, the Aboriginal and Torres Straits Islander Commission (ATSIC) that had presided over the continuing social disaster. This was followed in 2007 by the Northern Territory Emergency Response which saw a federal government taskforce take responsibility for the administration of the homelands. The Rudd Labor Government, elected in 2007, continued the previous government's policy of practical reconciliation approach by mainstreaming Indigenous services by means of the 'Close the Gap' strategy.

Rethinking of the separatist approach in the 2000s posed a grave threat to the existence of the Aboriginal industry. Little wonder that over the last decade Indigenous leaders and organisations have devoted so much time and energy to promoting Indigenous recognition and the Voice.

This is about far more than mere symbolism. Advocates for the Voice intend that it should operate as a restraint on parliamentary power over Indigenous affairs. Likely political consequences of enshrinement of the Voice can also be gauged by the original Indigenous recognition proposal for a racial non-discrimination clause which would amount to a legal power of veto over jurisdiction of the Australian parliament regarding Indigenous affairs. And it is worth noting that the Uluru Statement actually demands recognition of sovereignty co-existing with the Australian Crown.

For the Aboriginal industry, the Voice represents a form of political protection against policy changes that would threaten the funding and future of its many organisations. There is every reason to think that the industry conceives of the Voice as a way of constitutionally guaranteeing both the institutional legacy of the policies of Aboriginal self-determination and the long-term future of remote communities.

The real world operation of the Voice would be liable to operate as an inherently political means of opposing government decisions and would, therefore, effectively resemble a third chamber of parliament. By functioning as the mouthpiece of the industry, the Voice would have a powerful and permanent position from which both to shape the political narrative around Indigenous affairs and to persuade parliament not to adopt policies deemed to be against Indigenous interests because the measures were considered to be unfair and discriminatory.

Such demands would inevitably be backed up not only by the political force of the Voice being a constitutionally-enshrined representative body but by the moral intimidation of claims of racism. Any reluctance by Parliament to listen to the Voice would be sure to generate accusations of a return to pre-Voice days and to colonial times of the paternalistic administration of Indigenous affairs.

By these means, the operation of the Voice would only serve to entrench in the Constitution the separatist approach to Indigenous affairs.

The never-ending claims made by the Aboriginal industry, taken up in the rhetoric of the conservative case, is that lack of Indigenous control over policy is responsible for the appalling state of Indigenous communities. But such claims are a time-honoured political tactic (as well as a power and funding grab) drawn straight from the playbook of the Aboriginal industry which seeks continued funding of Aboriginal-controlled services. It is the Aboriginal industry that will be empowered by the Voice at the expense of the most disadvantaged Indigenous Australians in remote communities.

Realist historical accounts tell us how forms of separatism have a long history in Indigenous policy, stretching from the formation of the Aboriginal missions in the 19th century to the ascendancy of Aboriginal self-determination in the 1970s. What unites these otherwise different social experiments is that all were based on the notion that Aborigines needed to be treated differently. As Helen Hughes explained in her landmark examination of the dire social conditions of the homelands, *Lands of Shame*, published in 2007:

> Aborigines and Torres Strait Islanders have been discriminated against by being treated differently for more than 200 years. It is not true that various policies have been tried and have failed. Policies have always been discriminatory, treating Aborigines and Torres Strait Islanders differently from other Australians. Sadly the most damaging discrimination in Australia's history has been the exceptionalism of the last 30 years that was intended to make up for past mistreatment. It has widened the gap between Indigenous and mainstream Australians in critical respects.

For 50 years, the lives of Indigenous Australians have been sacrificed in the name of the separatist experiment with Aboriginal self-determination that, to the nation's shame, has ill-served the most excluded members of Australian society.

The aim of Indigenous policy in the 21st century should be to give all Indigenous Australians the same opportunities as other Australians. The Voice will not achieve this. Instead, it will almost certainly entrench politically the failed self-determination agenda of the 1970s and, with it, the disadvantage that that experiment has entrenched.

Conservatism and 'Lost Generations'

Some conservative advocates of the Voice appear to be attempting to alleviate 'settler's guilt' – an inherited disquiet that unequal prosperity between Indigenous and some non-Indigenous Australians must be attributed to the historic destruction of

Aboriginal society. A more generous account of their motivation might be that they want Australia to take responsibility for the past, present, and future of a nation in which Indigenous people can claim their rightful place. Their goal of a reconciled nation is right and proper; the means they endorse to achieve this are misguided and counter-productive.

Responsibility for the morally dubious promise that the present will make to the future by enshrining the Voice in the Constitution will lie with those who are now campaigning for a successful referendum outcome. But the true burden will be borne by the future 'lost generations' of Indigenous Australians who will be destined to remain an underclass trapped in dysfunctional circumstances and communities for life, for want of the jobs, education, and other opportunities necessary for success in mainstream Australia.

One might argue that those Indigenous Australians who remain locked out of mainstream society have suffered from too much, rather than too little, political attention during the last half century when self-determination has dominated Indigenous affairs. Indigenous suffering will not be ended by implementing another political solution, such as the Voice. Rather, the aim should be to take the politics out of Indigenous affairs so that the welfare of some Indigenous Australians is no longer sacrificed to the pursuit of the separatist dream that has long turned into a nightmare.

Genuinely addressing the shameful, intolerable, and fundamentally un-Australian situation that has left the most disadvantaged Indigenous Australians to suffer as the victims of the political ideology of self-determination should be dominating discussion of Indigenous affairs. The debate about the future direction of Indigenous policy should be concerned with how to end, rather than perpetuate, Aboriginal separatism.

Yet this is the debate that an Indigenous Voice enshrined in the Australian Constitution will make far more difficult for the nation to have. Failure to understand this is the flaw lying at the heart of the supportive conservative case which will result not in reconciliation but in prolonging the separatist nightmare.

Suggested reading

Helen Hughes, *Lands of shame : Aboriginal and Torres Strait Islander 'Homelands' in Transition*, (Centre for Independent Studies: St Leonards, NSW, 2007).

Peter Sutton, *The Politics of Suffering : Indigenous Australia and The End of the Liberal Consensus*, Melbourne University Press: Melbourne, VIC, 2009).

Gary Johns, *Aboriginal self-determination: The Whiteman's Dream*, (Connor Court: Ballarat, VIC, 2011).

6

THE INDIGENOUS VOICE DOES NOT SPEAK FOR COUNTRY

Nyunggai Warren Mundine AO

There's a saying: we have two ears and one mouth so we can listen twice as much as we speak. In my family, it was two ears, two eyes and one mouth. From my earliest memories, I was taught to use my ears to listen and my eyes to observe and research before using my mouth to ask questions, talk and discuss ideas.

I used to sit and listen to the old people, my grandparents, parents, uncles, aunties, older siblings, and cousins. There was adult talk and there was children talk. Children were expected to listen and learn.

I learnt that only countrymen and women speak for country. It's our culture. I can't speak for someone else's country. Only they can speak for their country. I can only speak for my country.

My people, my ancestors, on my father's side, are Bundjalung. Our country runs from the Clarence River (Berrinbah) New South Wales, in the south, to Beenleigh, Queensland in the north. My mother's side are Gumbaynggirr people of the Nambucca and Yuin people from Moruya NSW, as well as the Irish, from County Cork. I was brought up with my Goori (Aboriginal) culture and my

Catholic faith from my Irish ancestry.

I have a photo as a wallpaper and screen saver on my computer. It's a black and white photo, taken around the end of the First World War. The photo is of a gathering of my ancestors at Baryulgil. In the photo is my father's father (ngadjang), Beygal Harry Mundine, and in his arms is a baby, my father (mahmung), Julang Roy Mundine. Next to ngadjang, is my father's mother (gami), Lillian Donnelly. My ngadjang and gami are surrounded by their grandparents, brothers, sisters, and cousins. In the front row at the feet of my ngadjang are my father's brothers, who are also my mahmung.

Every time I use my computer, the photo reminds me of Mundine-jali, my Mundine mob of Wehlubal and Baryulgil clans. My djagun, my country. Where I fit in the universe. Where I come from. The name 'Mundine' comes from my great great grandfather, who was known as Mundi then Harry Mundi and finally as Harry Mundine.

Recently I was in Canberra for the opening of the Commonwealth Parliament to see the swearing in and hear the maiden speeches of new Indigenous members of Parliament.

That same week I travelled to Gulkula, in east Arnhem Land, for the 2022 Garma Festival. I have a kinship relationship with the Yolngu people of the area through my brother who lived and worked there for over two decades. Through that kinship relationship Yolgnu country is like my home. I attended at Garma there as the Chairman of the Australian Indigenous Education Foundation (AIEF). I also went to hear what the Prime Minister, Anthony Albanese, had to say about the Uluru Statement from the Heart and his plan for a referendum on the Indigenous Voice to Parliament.

I have been a long-time campaigner for Indigenous rights in education, economic prosperity, civil rights and equity, land rights, native title, business development, reduction of crime and better health.

The PM announced that the constitutional amendments for the Australian public to consider at referendum will be the addition of three new clauses:

1. There shall be a body to be called the Aboriginal and Torres Strait Islander Voice.

2. The Aboriginal and Torres Strait Islander Voice may make representations to Parliament and the executive government on matters relating to Aboriginal and Torres Strait Islander peoples.

3. The Parliament shall, subject to this constitution, have powers to make laws with respect to the composition, functions, powers, and procedures of the Aboriginal and Torres Strait Islander Voice.

The referendum question will be a simple, *"Do you support an alteration to the Constitution that establishes an Aboriginal and Torres Strait Islander Voice?"*

In 2017, a gathering of 250 Indigenous Australians met at the Yulara Resort, a short distance from Uluru, as the First Nations National Constitutional Convention to discuss how Indigenous Australians would be recognised in the Australian Constitution. The Convention took place over four days and at the end delivered the 'Uluru Statement from the Heart' (see page ix).

During the Convention, a small group of delegates, who reject constitutional recognition as recognising an occupying power and instead demand a sovereign treaty, walked out with a spokeswomen saying "It's not a dialogue, it's a one-way conversation. Every time we try and raise an issue our voices are silenced".

The Uluru Statement from the Heart called for real and practical change in Australia through the establishment of a constitutionally enshrined Voice to Parliament and the establishment of a

Makarrata Commission, to undertake processes of treaty-making and truth-telling.

Five years on from this process and there is still no consensus among Aboriginal and Torres Strait Islander peoples about whether the Uluru Statement is the way forward to settle the unfinished business arising from colonisation. Don't be blindly led into the belief that all Indigenous Australians support the Uluru Statement from the Heart and the Aboriginal and Torres Strait Islander Voice to Parliament.

Over the past five years, I've met with, and listened to, traditional owners from across the nation, including in Mutitjulu at the base of Uluru, who've told me they do not support the Uluru Statement from the Heart. That it is not our culture; it is the wrong way. That we are Australians, proud Australians. Most Indigenous people I meet and listen to are focused on practical outcomes such as less crime, more jobs, more business and economic development, better education and health outcomes, and increasing the number of elected members of local government and state, territory, and Commonwealth parliaments.

The symbolism of a Voice is not what is being asked for on Country. To make matters worse, no one seems to know, to understand, or be able to explain what the Voice or the Makarrata Commission are. And if they are able to, then, so far, they have been unwilling to do so. The Prime Minister has avoided detail on the Voice; instead he uses motherhood statements to justify its existence, such as it is "good manners".

Let's consider how the three proposed constitutional clauses creating the Voice, as well as the proposed Makarrata Commission, sit when looking at Aboriginal cultures and the sovereign liberal democratic Australian state.

At this stage, it must be pointed out that anyone who opposes either the Voice or the Makarrata Commission will have to battle against the wealthiest and most powerful people in Australia. Any opposition to these proposals will struggle to be heard against a media that has overwhelmingly signed on to the Voice to Parliament, and against large corporations and the enormously funded Indigenous industry.

After speaking with senior legal people, it seems each of the three points of the referendum proposal has a question mark over it.

> Point 1: *There shall be a body to be called the Aboriginal and Torres Strait Islander Voice.*

The issue here is the word "Voice". No one seems to know what that means under constitutional law. It does not appear in, nor has it been tested under, any constitution of a liberal democracy such as ours.

I've heard it said that putting the Voice into the Constitution is like putting the High Court into the Constitution. But there were hundreds of years of precedent and experience with courts and appeal courts that were known before the High Court was enshrined in our founding document.

The High Court is established under section 71 of the Constitution which says: *The judicial power of the Commonwealth shall be vested in a Federal Supreme Court, to be called the High Court of Australia, and in such other federal courts as the Parliament creates, and in such other courts as it invests with federal jurisdiction.* The most important phrases – "Supreme Court", "courts" and "judicial power" – were known concepts rooted in longstanding principles of Common Law and the Westminster system of government. No other constitution of a Cestern or Common Law nation has a 'Voice' in it.

Of our Commonwealth cousins, Canada's constitution includes

a simple statement in section 35(1) that "the existing aboriginal and treaty rights of the aboriginal people of Canada are hereby recognised and affirmed".

In New Zealand, Maori peoples are not mentioned in the constitution, but the Treaty of Waitangi Act (1975) established the Waitangi Tribunal and gave the Treaty of Waitangi recognition in New Zealand law. Importantly, these laws of recognition are based on treaties – that is, agreements between each of those countries and its first peoples.

> Point 2: *The Aboriginal and Torres Strait Islander Voice may make representations to Parliament and the executive government on matters relating to Aboriginal and Torres Strait Islander peoples.*

In this point, the word "matters" is the concern. The word means 'everything'. Indigenous Australians are Australian citizens. There is no law, regulation or policy, nor any act or decision of the Federal government or parliament, that doesn't relate to Aboriginal and Torres Strait Islander people. Energy. Mining. Tax. Defence. National security. Trade and commerce. Health. Education. Foreign affairs. All are 'matters' relating to Aboriginal and Torres Strait Islander peoples.

> Point 3: *The Parliament shall, subject to this Constitution, have powers to make laws with respect to the composition, functions, powers, and procedures of the Aboriginal and Torres Strait Islander Voice.*

This doesn't confer any new powers on the Parliament. The Parliament has this power under the Constitution to set up a Voice today, and could do so and save the nearly $200 million set aside for a referendum. The Voice could be immediately established with those funds and begin achieving the promised real outcomes for Indigenous Australians.

What's intended to come after the Voice is equally important. The aim of the Makarrata Commission is "to supervise a process of agreement making between governments and First Nations and truth-telling about our history".

The word "Makarrata" is Yolngu Matha which the Uluru Statement from the Heart describes as meaning "the coming together after a struggle". At its most literal meaning, Makarrata has been described by Yolngu woman, Merrikiyawuy Ganambarr-Stubbs, as, "a spear penetrating, usually the thigh, of a person that has done wrong... so that they cannot hunt anymore, that they cannot walk properly, that they cannot run properly; to maim them, to settle them down, to calm them—that's Makarrata". The spearing of someone who has done wrong is a traditional form of conflict resolution and settling disputes.

Dealing with what's described as the "truth-telling about our history" scares me. Is the Makarrata Commission going to be pushing its own version of history? Is it going to override curriculum boards and universities? Or the research by organisations like the AIATSIS, or the huge body of research undertaken in support of native title claims and claims to recover stolen wages? Why does truth-telling about history need to be supervised at all, let along by some big bureaucratic commission? This is Big Brother stuff.

The first part of the stated aims of the Commission – "to supervise a process of agreement making between governments and First Nations" – is also worrying. Australia's 'first nations' are the traditional owner groups, like the Bundjalung, the Gumbaynggirr, Yuin and Yolngu peoples. A treaty is an agreement between a government and a traditional owner group. So the Makarrata Commission would assume the role of supervising treaty conversations and negotiations between governments and traditional owners.

Note the reference to "governments" in the plural. Several state and territory governments are already in discussions with traditional owners about treaties. The Liberal Party position on treaties has long been that it is a state and territory matter because those governments have jurisdiction over land rights and native title.

When these agreements are made with traditional owners, we'll see what is left for the Commonwealth to do with a Makarrata Commission. Or is the intention that the Makarrata Commission will assume supervision of these discussions too? I don't see why we need a centralised bureaucracy sitting over the top of all treaty conversations and negotiations across the country at every level of government.

Another type of agreement between traditional owner groups and governments are the native title agreements mostly entered into with state and territory governments. These are currently made directly between the relevant government and a native title claimant group (constituted through a prescribed body corporate) which receives legal and other expert advice that may be provided by a native title services corporation or by other advisers.

Once an agreement has been reached, it can be brought before the Native Title Tribunal and registered through the Federal Court. Presumably, a Makarrata Commission would supervise all of this. What will that supervision entail? Do the proponents of the Uluru Statement from the Heart envisage the Makarrata Commission representing or speaking for traditional owner groups in native title claims and negotiations? Will it become some kind of native title gatekeeper? I believe most traditional owners would find that unacceptable.

Conversations and negotiations between governments and traditional owners, on any subject, do not need supervision by a huge bureaucracy or to be brokered by an intermediary body.

The Makarrata Commission would be an unnecessary shadow governance body. And we don't need it. Through the native title process we already have representative organisations tied to traditional owner groups. For any traditional owner groups who don't have recognised native title or a native title claim, there's no reason they can't also have a representative body. All the information and data required to identify Australia's traditional owner groups – their language, their country, their land and their eligible members – is already available. Representative bodies could be established for every one of them based on the native title model.

The Voice and Makarrata Commission both sound to me like more bureaucracy controlling Indigenous lives and bossing us around. A key objective of the 1967 referendum was to dismantle the state and territory boards, and the protection boards that controlled Aboriginal and Torres Strait Islander lives on a day-to-day basis. It seems to me we're just going to create new ones. These huge bureaucracies will also involve more expense and will mean that fewer resources will get to where they are needed – that is, outside Canberra, in regional and remote areas.

Under my Goori culture, (Bundjalung, Gumbaynggirr and Yuin), only people of the country can speak for their country. I can't speak for other people's country. Where is the voice for the men and women on country? How do they fit into the Voice and the Makarrata Commission? These traditional owners seem to be the forgotten people.

Traditional owners should be their own voice for their own nation and country. They don't need some new national Voice or a Makarrata Commission to speak for them. They need the Government to listen and go talk to them through their own representative bodies. The Yolngu and Torres Strait Islander peoples have very effectively petitioned governments and made their voices heard over decades through their representative systems and bodies based on their own culture and kinship systems.

The Yolngu Nations Assembly (YNA), for example, is an organisation created for engagement between the Yolngu people and the Australian and Northern Territory governments with structure and governance based on customary law and traditional regional and clan representation. The YNA is recognised by Yolngu people and speaks for Yolngu country. Through their own organisation and leadership, Yolngu people speak with one the loudest voices of any group of Australians to parliaments and governments. In 2015, then Co-Convenor of Yolngu National Assembly, Matthew Dhulumburrk Gaykamaŋu, said:

> We want a treaty because right now we get directives just from the government side for housing, education, skills training. This is one-sided talk that never ends in things that work. Government needs to listen to Yolngu thinking for Yolngu problems. A treaty is good because we need a foundational agreement for the Australian government and the Yolngu government, before anything else happens.

A day after the Prime Minister's announcement about the Voice in Garma, Yingiya Mark Guyula, a Yolngu man and the independent member for the Northern Territory electoral division of Mulka which covers a large part of Yolngu country, made the following comments:

> Voice itself, it's hopeless it's not much at all. It's not good enough, that's not what we want. People here don't want voice, we want voice included into treaty, and we want truth-telling into treaty.

> Through a treaty we want to say, no we don't want that policy, we don't want your policy, you listen to us.

On 23 August 2022, Torres Strait Islander representatives signed *The Masig Statement – Malungu Yangu Wakay (Voice from the Deep)*. The Statement called for self-determination, the right to freely determine political status, and to pursue economic, social and cultural development, autonomy, or self-government, in matters relating to internal and local affairs, and partnerships with regional stakeholders, and with the Queensland and federal governments to achieve the region's goals and aspirations. Torres Strait Island Regional Council Mayor, Phillemon Mosby said:

> The Masig Statement is a mandate from the people for the leaders of our region to stand together in unity. We see that voice to parliament and constitutional change will give our voice a unique place in this country.

Listen and observe what is being said here. These are not calls for an 'Aboriginal' or an 'Indigenous' voice; or for 'Indigenous' or even 'Aboriginal and Torres Strait Islander' self-determination; or for a treaty with 'Aboriginal' or 'Indigenous' people. The call is for "Yolngu thinking for Yolngu problems." A voice to parliament and constitutional change will provides a place for "our voice", a Torres Strait Islander voice.

If Yolngu people settle a treaty with the Australian or Northern Territory governments it will be negotiated and signed by Yolngu leaders speaking for Yolngu country. And they won't be told what to agree by a Makarrata Commission. Torres Strait Islander people want self-determination and self-government on matters relating to Torres Strait Islander country.

If the Voice makes a representation to Parliament that doesn't have the support of Yolngu people or Torres Strait Islander people, then it won't be their voice. I don't believe any Aboriginal or Torres Strait Islander people will regard the Voice as being able to speak for them or their country. Any proposal for representative bodies or treaty making will fail to deliver results if the traditional owner groups are not central.

I am supportive of recognising and acknowledging Australia's indigenous peoples in the Constitution. But let's not pretend Aboriginal and Torres Strait Islander people aren't able to make representations and be heard by governments or parliaments already.

Following the 2022 federal election, we have more Indigenous members in the Commonwealth Parliament than ever before. We have our second Indigenous Minister for Indigenous Australians. Six out of eight states and territories have initiated treaty processes.

For decades, Indigenous people and Indigenous organisations have been lobbying and making representation to governments and parliaments on matters that concern them. When I go to Canberra I'm always tripping over blackfellas walking through the corridors of Parliament on their way to meeting with ministers, backbenchers, opposition members and crossbenchers. Ministers and prime ministers have appointed Indigenous advisory committees. Oppositions also consult with, and take advice from, Indigenous people and organisations.

Since 1973 we've had four elected Indigenous bodies – the National Aboriginal Consultative Committee (NACC), the National Aboriginal Conference, ATSIC and the National Congress of Australia's First Peoples. Most saw low voting participation.

NACC was set up as an advisory body but soon developed a new constitution giving itself autonomy, policy-making, and administrative powers. It didn't survive. We've also had advisory bodies like the Council for Aboriginal Reconciliation, the National Indigenous Council, The Prime Ministers' Indigenous Advisory Council, and the Coalition of the Peaks.

Yet here we go again. Einstein is credited with saying, "insanity is doing the same thing over and over and expecting different results." Isn't it time that we did something different? Like empowering local traditional owner organisations with governance, and empowering Indigenous individuals through businesses, economic development, and education?

Self-determination and empowerment mean taking responsibility for yourself, your family, and your community; making your own decisions and controlling your own destiny; earning your own money, being self-sufficient and supporting yourself and your family without government dependency or bureaucratic oversight.

My grandparents, parents, aunties, and uncles lived most of their lives as second-class citizens but in their own minds they weren't. None of them waited for government to do anything. They made their own decisions and took responsibility for their own lives. They worked hard, got as much education and skills as possible, and ensured their children went to school and were educated. My parents owned their own home as did my mother's parents, and my father's people had their own land at Baryulgil.

There can be no self-determination or autonomy for any community if there is total dependence on governments and bureaucracies, or if there is no real economy. No country or community can survive without an economy to support it. The greatest threat to Indigenous Australians living on country remote and regional Australia is chronic dependence on government without needing meaningfully to contribute in return.

Empowerment and self-determination come from economic participation – having a job or running your own business, and having the education and skills to do that. Real empowerment for traditional owners living on country will come from community members having the skills and training to do the jobs and provide the goods and services for those communities that are currently provided by people who come from outside the community, or are not provided at all.

Policies that support empowerment are those that support getting children to school and adults into jobs and businesses. One example is the Federal Government's Indigenous Procurement Policy (IPP), launched on the 1 July 2015.

Simply put, the policy requires that three per cent of government contracts are awarded for Indigenous-owned businesses. Mandatory set-aside rules require that for contracts in remote areas and small contracts (to the value of $80,000 – $200,000) no tender is required if an Indigenous-owned business can demonstrate value-for-money. Indigenous employment and business participation targets also apply to prime contractors for contracts awarded in certain categories.

In the year before the IPP, government contracts worth less than $7 million were awarded to Indigenous owned businesses. Since the launch of the policy, contracts worth over $5.3 billion have been awarded to 2,603 Indigenous businesses. Private, commercial, and Indigenous owned businesses, that hire and train Indigenous workers are the way forward.

The Indigenous Procurement Policy was based on the success of the mining and resources industry in establishing Indigenous business contracts and employment. Fortescue Metals Group's Billion Opportunities program has awarded more than $4 billion in contracts and sub-contracts alone to Indigenous owned businesses since the initiative was launched in 2011.

It's not rocket science to work out that countries around the world which have private, commercial, and profitable businesses, as well as an educated population, have done more to lift people out of poverty so that they can enjoy healthier and longer lives, and enjoy all the opportunities and benefits of a prosperous nation.

The Voice to Parliament referendum and the proposals for constitutional change are an unneeded distraction and a waste of time and resources. If advocates for the Voice truly believe it will bring about real improvements for Indigenous Australians, call on Parliament to legislate it right now. Why wait? Answer all the doubts by proving the doubters wrong.

The Australian Constitution is not racist and does not need race-based privileges. Nor is it racist, or to stand 'on the wrong side of history', to oppose constitutional amendment. We need to defend our liberal democracy. Changes to our Constitution should only be for the benefit all Australians, and to safeguard the freedoms and civil rights of us all.

7

HEAD OVER HEART: THE LEGAL, DEMOCRATIC AND PRACTICAL PROBLEMS RAISED BY THE ULURU STATEMENT

Amanda Stoker

As is so often the case with radical ideas, academic enthusiasm is high for the proposal for an Indigenous "Voice" to Parliament. Too few of the legal, democratic and practical problems raised by the Uluru Statement from the Heart (see page ix) have been the subject of objective consideration by this class, and, as a consequence, the public debate so far has relied heavily on leveraging sincere feelings of goodwill of Australians for their Indigenous cousins.

However, any discussion of the implications of change both to Australia's constitution and its democratic institutions deserves a lot more "head" than "heart". This is because the proposals in the Uluru Statement cannot be considered to be in the interests of Australians as a whole, or Indigenous Australians as a part thereof.

Indeed, the proposal has the real prospect of doing substantial damage to social cohesion and democratic institutions without meaningfully improving the lives of the people it seeks to assist.

The Uluru Statement from the Heart, reproduced in full at the beginning of this book, is, indeed, a statement of emotional power. That emotional power, however, conceals several logical fallacies and concepts from the political extreme.

The shift to group identity

To cite incarceration rates and youth detention rates – both of which I agree are far too high – in isolation is to mislead. It is not mere racism that causes incarceration and detention. It is a complex web of social disfunction that manifests in individuals making choices to behave in a manner contrary to law. Government does not inflict this in the here and now, though there are many government policies that have, over time, been less than helpful. Indeed, taxpayers have never spent more trying to help Indigenous Australians out of situations of social disfunction and consequent disadvantage.

It does not follow from observation of incarceration and detention rates that an Indigenous Voice to parliament will resolve them either. Indeed, it smacks of the assumption that because some other things haven't worked, then this *must* be the answer.

What is significant about the inclusion of this information in the Uluru Statement is the way in which it shifts accountability for individuals' behaviour, accomplishments and life outcomes from the individuals involved to groups. The appeal to group identity is significant because it represents a shift away from a commitment to the fundamental equality of all humans who are to be regarded as individuals based on who they are and what they do – a commitment upon which our institutions rest.

Commitment to the fundamental equality of each individual is the organising principle of liberal democracies, the conceptual underpinning of the notion of human rights, and, in my view, the only truly non-racist position because race is never relevant to human worth.

In contrast, group identity, also known as identity politics, ties human value to external attributes, often outside the individual's control. These are usually race, sex, sexuality or more recently fashionable notions of gender identity.

When group identity is the organising principle, individuals don't bear *any* responsibility for their part in the decisions that have led to their life outcomes.

When group identity is the organising principle, it conceals the absurdity of demanding that descendants of those who inflicted a certain wrong in the past compensate the descendants of those who were wronged.

Political systems that are based on group identity have perverse incentives. By prioritising for advantage those who are perceived to have suffered past wrongs as a group, those who are members are rewarded for leaning into victimhood, rather than for prevailing over their circumstances.

Further, the incentive to identify as a part of group victimised by another group drives a tribalism that threatens broader social cohesion. When individuals are valued based on genetic attributes over which they have no control, rather than on the content of their character, we fundamentally devalue the good nature and good works of all humans.

This is not to say it is wrong to enjoy and practice the different cultures that make up this nation. Our differences make this country richer. It is simply to say that the fundamental organising principle of our nation must be that we are all Australians who bear equal rights in every way, regardless of colour or creed.

Our culture and history are layers of the onion that make us different individuals within that nation. They should not be the basis for separating from the nation or for pitting one culture against another by affording them different rights.

To understand the different rights proposed by the Uluru Statement, it is necessary to consider the nature of the proposal in detail.

The changes proposed by the Uluru Statement

There are three core components to the Uluru Statement:

- Constitutional recognition (likely of sovereignty, although this is not absolutely clear);
- A constitutionally enshrined Indigenous Voice to parliament;
- A Makkarata Commission, charged with a process of "truth telling" and a process of "agreement making" with governments, also known as treaty-making.

These are extreme concepts and would dramatically change the social, institutional and legal landscape of this nation in a manner that I consider harmful to the nation as a whole, and to the Indigenous Australians it purports to assist. I will consider each of the three components in turn.

Constitutional recognition of sovereignty

The assertion of "sovereignty" in the Uluru Statement is a radical notion that sits in conflict with the approach that has evolved since the *Mabo* decision.[1] Yet by committing to the Uluru Statement in full, Labor, and much of corporate Australia, has

---

1   *Mabo and Others v Queensland (No. 2)* [1992] HCA 23; (1992) 175 CLR 1.

committed to recognising Aboriginal and Torres Strait Islander "sovereignty" over Australia.

According to the Uluru Statement, "this sovereignty is a spiritual notion" which has "never been ceded or extinguished, and co-exists with the sovereignty of the Crown".

There is no denying that Aboriginal and Torres Strait Islanders' were the first inhabitants of our island continent. Most Australians accept and respect the ongoing connection Indigenous Australians have with the land. But couching this "spiritual connection" in the language of sovereignty fundamentally distorts the meaning of the term.

Sovereignty is not a term that denotes a spiritual, historical or emotional connection with a place. It denotes supreme legal authority over a given territory. It is the power of the government to exercise authority over Australia's institutions, to pass laws, and to enforce them.

By definition, the sovereignty of a nation-state cannot "co-exist" with the sovereignty of others. The closest thing possible is delegation, such as for state governments that operate within a federation.

For it to have any meaning, it would have to go beyond the current native title system. That system, which is the *product* of Australian sovereignty, has developed to take account of conflicting rights and uses of land, such as pastoral leases and mining licenses.

One only needs to consider the long list of unanswered questions that the concept raises to know that constitutional recognition of sovereignty would make a mess of a nuanced system of native title.

How much will recognising Indigenous claims to sovereignty change this delicate balance of native title law, carefully crafted over decades to ensure balance between the property rights of all? What will it do to current systems of title and private property ownership rights? Will it remove the certainty needed for major mining and minerals projects to proceed where traditional owner approval has already been provided? What will the status be of the generous payments already agreed, or made, to Indigenous communities as compensation for the impact on native title of such activity? No one has even attempted to engage with these issues.

When the High Court recognised native title in *Mabo*, it did not do so on the basis of Indigenous sovereignty over Australia. By a majority, it recognised a form of native title which, in the cases where it had not been extinguished, reflects the entitlement of Australia's Indigenous inhabitants, in accordance with their laws or customs, to their traditional lands as a form of permissive occupancy at the will of the Crown.

Put another way, there was nothing in the decision that first recognised native title, nor in the *Native Title Act* that followed, to suggest that native title lands should be considered as anything but a part of the sovereign Australian nation.

The High Court's formulation was one which recognised the rights of traditional owners without dividing the nation into two or more separate sovereign bodies on the basis of their racial or cultural background.

That was quite proper, both on the basis of the meaning of the term and with an eye to Australian cohesion. Anything else would have amounted to granting authority that the lands over which native title was established could cede from the Commonwealth of Australia.

In none of the major cases dealing with native title since has there been a finding, or even a comment in *obiter dicta*, that the rights of

Indigenous Australians to land amounts to recognition of, or is the product of, sovereignty.

Even in the most recent major case dealing with native title jurisprudence, *Northern Territory v Griffiths*[2] (known as the *Timber Creek* decision) – which awarded substantial compensation for the loss of the economic value of traditional lands, as well as acknowledging the cultural significance of the loss of Aboriginal connection to those lands – there was neither an assertion of, nor a finding of, Aboriginal sovereignty.

Again, the answer lies in properly articulating the problem that policy changes are attempting to solve. Native title policy cannot turn back the clock to undo history. And while there is no doubt that there are aspects of European settlement that have visited disadvantage upon Indigenous Australians, there are also many advantages – I would suggest many more and more significant advantages.

But however one views this aspect of history, there is no evidence by which we could reasonably expect this formulation of so-called "sovereignty" to lead to better life outcomes for Indigenous Australians. That is true whether measures are based on health standards, education levels, incarceration rates or the incidence of family violence.

If as a nation we want to see changes to native title policy that are more economically and culturally empowering for traditional owners, there is merit in developing a framework for more readily developing and extracting livelihoods from traditional lands in a manner driven by and supported by those owners.

It should bother all Australians that community-wide structures of ownership prevent traditional owners from getting a mortgage to buy or build their own home on the lands over which they

---

2   *Northern Territory v Griffiths* [2019] HCA 7; (2019) 269 CLR 1

have native title. Yet we know that home ownership is one of the most successful mechanisms for intergenerational improvement in living standards, wealth and opportunity.

Similarly, successive governments have poured taxpayer support for economic development into remote communities. But the real barrier to being able to get finance to start or develop a business in these areas is the communal nature of land ownership.

It should be possible to allow individual communities to develop structures for making their native title more meaningful and more readily leveraged, and that reflect the nature of their particular cultural needs and their economic and other priorities. But this does not necessitate constitutional recognition of "sovereignty".

Indeed, to afford such recognition, within any sensible meaning of the term, would necessarily carve our country into pieces based on racial and cultural connections. This, in turn, would leave the land mass we call Australia divided, physically and socially, and weakened in its defence and economic power to the point at which it would face substantial strategic vulnerability.

A constitutionally enshrined Indigenous Voice to Parliament

The proposal for a constitutionally enshrined Indigenous Voice to Parliament suffers from several weaknesses, any one of which provides sufficient cause for it to be shelved.

First, it assumes all Indigenous Australians think alike. That's not just false, it's downright racist. As the divergent views of serving Aboriginal politicians Linda Burney, Senator Lidia Thorpe and Senator Jacinta Nampijinpa Price suggest, Aboriginal people do not have homogenous views.

The interests of Indigenous Australians will vary with their personal experience, their family experience, the history of their tribe, and more ordinary differences like whether they live in the city, the regions or in remote Australia, whether or not they work, whether they are parents, and the beliefs that underpin their politics.

Second, it fundamentally usurps the democratic institutions that ensure all people in this nation have the same legal and political rights. The Australian Parliament, as it currently stands, belongs to Indigenous Australians as much as any other Australian. Indeed, people of Aboriginal background are represented there in numbers exceeding their proportion of the population. That is to be celebrated not just because it ensures the experience of Indigenous Australians is relevant to the policy-making process for the nation, but also because it shows that the wider electorate values these representatives for their substance and not solely because of their group identity. Sadly, a racially constituted body would not have that strength.

Whether it is crafted as binding or advisory, any Indigenous Voice would have the effect of adding a layer of delay and bureaucracy to a democratic process that is already inflexible and slow. That will be exacerbated if its procedures are to be consensus-driven, for there are many subjects on which reasonable and decent people can disagree.

To allow one racial group to veto laws or policy that are otherwise reflective of the will of all Australians – albeit through the messy process we call democracy – is apt to drive resentment and division. Even if it is framed as advisory rather than binding, Prime Minister Anthony Albanese has candidly observed that "it would be a brave government" that didn't follow its findings. If the political pressure on the government or executive were such that they were penalised politically for divergence with its findings, the practical effect will be identical to a veto.

Third, there has been little engagement about what should be the remit of any body of this kind. Proponents have, somewhat vaguely, suggested it will be for laws and policies affecting Indigenous Australians. Well, the basic needs of Indigenous people are not inherently different to any other human beings.

To say that it's limited to native title and cultural heritage laws is so narrow as to disrespect the depth and complexity of Indigenous Australians.

Tax laws, environmental laws, the Corporations Act, education and health policy, laws supporting research and development, relationships with state and territory governments and much more, all impact upon the lives of Indigenous Australians. If they fall within the remit of the Voice, as has been foreshadowed, you can expect less speed and more bureaucracy from government.

There's not much that should be off the table if a body of this kind is going to truly cover the areas of law and policy that are relevant to Indigenous Australians' lives. And yet if we were to create such a body, we would make it even slower, more expensive, and less commercially viable to get projects off the ground in Australia.

The net effect would be to make Australia less desirable as a place to invest. That might not sound like a big deal, but its practical effect is to make fewer the jobs, particularly in the mining sector, on which so many Indigenous communities depend. If there is one issue on which the various perspectives on Indigenous policy agree it is that high quality jobs are vital to transforming remote communities from dangerous and disfunctional to healthy, safe and productive. It is perverse that an Indigenous voice could make that harder than ever to achieve.

Fourth, there is uncertainty about the impact that an Indigenous Voice would have upon the finality of the decisions of parliament.

There is the very real risk that if an Indigenous voice is constitutionally entrenched, decisions of executive governments and parliaments could be subject to applications to the courts seeking review on the basis of failing adequately to have had regard to the needs of Indigenous communities.

Fifth, there is a dearth of evidence to suggest that this is what is needed to deliver the improvement in life outcomes that is the stated purpose of such a body.

And while this proposal is much more radical than anything seen in any other jurisdiction worldwide, race-based bodies implemented in other countries, such as Canada, can hardly be considered to have been a resounding success.

A Makkarata Commission

Treaty

As with the notion of 'sovereignty', proposals for a treaty also suffer from many of the problems associated with treating Indigenous Australians as though they constitute another country

The purpose of treaties is not to effect feelings of peace with history. Treaties are for the making of agreements between sovereign nations. They can be used to implement the rules of an international order (such as maritime treaties and treaties to establish bodies like the International Court of Justice and the World Trade Organisation) or for the terms of concession of the conquered after war.

What we do know is that any so-called "treaty" process will come with a bill for compensation – one that taxpayers will be expected to pay.

And given that the High Court in *Timber Creek* ordered $1.3 million in damages for cultural loss, in a total judgment sum of $2,350,350 for economic and cultural loss over 127 hectares, and where that "loss" in large part comprised the provision of public infrastructure and services from which the traditional owners obtained some benefit, the total bill to be footed by the tax payer is likely to be eye-watering.

Again, compensation will not be awarded for a specific crime, in the way that members of the Stolen Generation have been compensated financially. Nor will it be for the loss of use of specific land, as was ordered in the *Timber Creek* case. Rather, it will be awarded to today's Indigenous person for harm inflicted upon long-deceased ancestors by the long-deceased ancestors of others. To blame those in the present for the actions of others in the past entrenches victimhood rather than empowerment.

It also marks a fundamental shift from a legal system based on individual responsibility for our actions to one of group grievance and responsibility.

Truth-telling

Our nation has come a long way in its collection, preservation and appreciation of Indigenous history, artifacts and art. That has enriched our nation greatly and will allow future generations of Indigenous people to have better connection to their heritage.

There is, however, a substantial risk carried by the notion of a "truth-telling" commission.

Inherent in the notion is the implication that our history, to this point, is somehow dishonest. It may be incompletely compiled or understood, but it is not false. It may not contain all of the necessary perspectives, but that does not mean that what we know now is a lie. That suggestion is unfair, and unproven.

Nevertheless, it is important that all with a story to share about Indigenous culture and its positive and negative interactions with non-Indigenous Australians, have an opportunity to do so.

The establishment of a body that would have as its mission the uncritical reception of so-called "evidence"; that would not test the reliability of that evidence (for it cannot be evidence of any value unless we are prepared to assess its veracity against other sources); and that would seek to elevate that evidence to the status of "truth" to the exclusion of other accounts is not just divisive; it is a recipe for the mangling of Indigenous and the settlers' history alike.

Conclusion

When I served on the Joint Select Committee on Constitutional Recognition of Indigenous People in the Australian Parliament, the course of submissions revealed that there was an absence of consensus among Indigenous communities about what the various proposals for constitutional recognition could achieve and indeed what their objectives were.

Some believed it would be an important symbol, others saw it as a vehicle for countering discrimination against Indigenous people. Some saw it as a part of the healing process for past wrongs, others saw it as a vehicle for treaty. Some saw it as a way to entrench a role for Indigenous people in government decision-making. There were, no doubt, even more objectives than those.

Throughout that time, and in the current debate, no one has properly addressed this fundamental question: what is the purpose of our Constitution?

If the purpose of our Constitution is to make us feel at peace with history, a model to insert a preamble might make sense (though I note the legal effect of a preamble is substantially more complex than mere symbolism).

If the purpose is to say something about our national identity, and the people, events and causes that make it up, then several of the amendment proposals might have value, though they carry the risk of empowering judicial activism.

But if the purpose of our Constitution is to allocate mechanically the powers and functions of a federal government and to define its relationship with the States – and that *is* its purpose – then the Uluru Statement is both radical and misconceived.

I do not deny that there is a deep emotional attachment to the idea of constitutional recognition in the hearts of many people. The difficulty is that the Constitution is not an emotional document; indeed, to insert emotion in a document with a legal purpose and operation is to invite judicial activism of the kind that did great harm to the concept of Australian citizenship in the decision of *Love and Thoms*[3].

I would support a proposal to amend the Constitution in a minimalist way. Abolition of Section 25 would be appropriate. That section contemplates the different treatment of Australians by the States on the basis of race for the purposes of voting, and is no longer used. Such an amendment would have moral force because it drives towards an Australia in which all citizens are treated equally. Indeed, that was the beauty of the 1967 referendum's amendments: it brought Indigenous people toward their rightful place as equal Australians.

I also support in principle amendment of Section 51(xxvi) so that it provides to the federal government a head of power sufficient

---

3   *Love and Thoms v Commonwealth* [2020] HCA 3

to provide support for existing native title legislation, but no more. The idea that we have a "race power" is inconsistent with the notion of the equality of Indigenous people. However, it is only in this narrow sense that I can support the constitutional recognition of Indigenous Australians.

In my view, an approach that puts at its centre the equal treatment of Indigenous people with other Australians will also have the best possible prospect of being accepted by the Australian people as a whole at a referendum.

If we are guided most prominently by the belief that Indigenous people deserve to be treated in all ways as equal to every other Australian, and by the belief that the constitution is a legal and mechanical, rather than a poetic or cultural, document, we will, as a nation, land in a place that is unifying, that enhances our institutions, and that pushes against the corrosive influence of group identity politics.

It would be a mistake to entrench any form of identity politics into our Constitution. It is far better to focus on the deep equality of Indigenous people, rather than seeking to elevate or separate them from other Australians.

As the role of constitutional amendments in the context of the rest of the Constitution are tested by individual cases, and the words of the Constitution are considered against a background of changing economic or cultural circumstances, judicial interpretation often leads to consequences unintended at the time of drafting. It means we should be very cautious about each and every word that is inserted, changed or deleted. It provides a good reason to maintain a narrow and legal purpose for the Constitution, and avoid adapting it to symbolic, emotional or cultural purposes.

The Uluru Statement seeks to do something of a deeply radical nature to Australian culture, its cohesion and its institutions, without any clear evidence that it would meaningfully improve the life outcomes of the people it seeks to help.

None of this is to deny the need to do more to close the gap between Indigenous and non-Indigenous Australians. State and federal governments have made progress, but life expectancy remains too short, domestic violence rates too high, rates of education and employment too low. And we should never be satisfied until every little Indigenous boy and girl born in remote communities can live safely in childhood, and grow to learn, earn and aspire to their goals.

Yet the beauty of the Australian nation – the sovereign Australian nation – is that it embraces us all and does not seek to divide us on the basis of our race, sex, colour or ethnicity.

There is a real risk that despite the good intentions of its proponents, the Uluru Statement will in fact deliver enduring obstacles to the economic advancement of Indigenous communities without offering any meaningful improvement to their lives.

8

IT'S OK FOR LIBERALS (AND ANYONE ELSE) TO SAY 'NO' TO INDIGENOUS RECOGNITION IN THE CONSTITUTION

Scott Prasser

Vote n. – a *formal expression of a choice between two or more candidates or courses of action, expressed typically through a ballot.*

Referendum n. – *a general vote by the electorate on a single political question which has been referred to them for a direct decision.*

The New Oxford Dictionary of English, (Oxford: OUP, 1998)

Introduction

Proposals are now under way for a referendum to enshrine in the Australian Constitution some sort of recognition of Aboriginal people. Details remain unclear at time of writing (November 2022).

This chapter will not consider the specific arguments for or against such a proposal; other contributors are covering that issue in detail. Rather, this chapter focusses on whether the constitutional and legislative issues with regard to changing the Australian Constitution allow for voters not only to be able to choose 'No' in the privacy of the ballot booth, but also to be adequately informed in order to exercise that choice.

The issue, as the definitions above highlight, is that to vote, whether in a general election or in a referendum, means having the ability to exercise choice. At an election, it is choice about a candidate, a party, and policy. Voters can accept or reject candidates. Both during an election and long before it, they can criticise a government or an opposition's policies, they can also call for some existing measures to be reversed and abolished. Voters' views can be motivated by genuine concern, by evidence as to its deleterious effects, or by personal prejudice, or just self-interest. The motives might come to light in subsequent debates; it is important that proposed alternative positions are not automatically rejected, or the proponents 'silenced' because they are regarded as somehow being unacceptable.

Similarly, choice is exercised in a referendum, where voters have to select 'Yes' or 'No' in response to the proposed question. In a liberal democracy, a referendum does not simply afford the opportunity to endorse a government's preferred option. That is what can happen under authoritarian regimes which use plebiscites – and employ a number of techniques – to secure high levels of support for the regime's actions. Authoritarian governments use plebiscites to proclaim the popular support by 'the people'. In a democracy, by contrast, voting 'No' remains a genuine option. The motives for making a particular decision a referendum can be the same as when voting in elections – that is, motives can be well -meaning and rational, or selfish and crass. The point is that a voter can still express a negative vote.

So, this chapter explores the right to say 'No' and also investigates how the exercise of this right is affected by a range of constitutional, legislative, and other political factors, such as accepted conventions, and past practice. For many people, the importance of allowing dissenting views to be heard and not suffocated in a referendum campaign is paramount. All this brings into focus the issue of how citizens become informed during modern election or referendum campaigns.

The nature of modern campaigning and informed decision-making

It is generally accepted that most voters lack detailed knowledge about specific policies or even about candidates in their electorate when they cast their vote at a general election. Few now join political parties or attend political meetings. Instead, voters take what are often referred to as 'information short cuts' when making decisions, relying on trusted sources of information – such as family, friends, workmates, general media outlets, interest groups of which they are members or which they support, political parties, and, increasingly, social media.

Some of these 'trusted' sources have a vested interest in supporting particular candidates or policies. In other cases, information on topics may be distorted or just plain wrong or simplistic. There will be exaggerations and distortions about what policies might or might not do and the fate that awaits a nation if one party wins and the other loses.

In relation to the forthcoming referendum about constitutional recognition and enshrining a Voice in the Constitution, it is probably safe to assume that most voters have not given the matter a great deal of attention. Polls indicate that voters are primarily concerned with other issues, such as cost of living pressures, interest rates, and holding on to jobs.

This means that the way the issues are now being discussed by the media and those other institutions with which voters connect or learn about will already be affecting popular perceptions about the referendum proposal. Where there is little detail, as is the present case, voters will hear largely emotional arguments in favour of the proposal. Those who publicly espouse a 'No' position are smaller in number and are often seen to be strident in their arguments; thus they tend to be sidelined by the media.

Moreover, as discussed later, given that referendum proposals can only be put by the government of the day, government is in the box seat and can therefore set the tone of the debate, allay fears, and promote the proposal before the referendum campaign even begins. Continuous campaigning is now the order of the day both in relation to elections and, increasingly, to referendum campaigns. Incumbent governments have available many resources and techniques that allow them to set the agenda. These include announcements by ministers, appointments to advisory committees, allocation of grants, and, as we know, even paid advertisements. Also, by virtue of being in office, governments can exert considerable influence on a wide range of opinion and thought leaders, including those in business, education and community services. These leaders can be called upon to make statements in support of a question proposed for a referendum.

So, let's be clear: the 'Yes' campaign for this referendum has already started. Indeed, it has been going on for some time. Meanwhile, because of the lack of details and the sensitivity that has formed around Aboriginal issues across a range of areas, the 'No' campaign has not effectively even started. The 'No' campaign does not yet know what it is up against; and it is even ambivalent about the legitimacy or appropriateness of voicing its opposition. All this has important ramifications for how the national referendum debate will play out once the official campaign starts. The issue is whether informed decision-making about the referendum question is possible if there is no 'No' case which is articulated strongly, loudly, and without restraint.

Informed decision-making in a referendum

Indeed, concerns about informed decision-making in relation to a referendum to change the Constitution are seen as being more important than those relating to a general election.

At a general election, the issues are wide, the promises many, and the specifics few. Moreover, evidence of what one policy will do is often thin on the ground, highly contested, and full of exaggeration and hyperbole.

Voters understand this and use their 'information shortcuts' to assess what is being promised and to evaluate their own situations before taking a punt on candidate X or party Y. They know if they get it too wrong, there will be another election in three or four years' time when they can throw out the existing government. And of course, they might also wonder if it really does matter because of the great similarities between the major parties; and those politicians are all cast from the same mould, aren't they?

Changing a constitution, and especially the Australian Constitution, is different from just changing a government. It has very long-lasting implications. Once done, it cannot easily be undone, at least in the Australian context. There has never been an amendment to reverse an earlier successful amendment to the Australian Constitution. In some national jurisdictions, amendment simply requires passage of a new law by the legislature. For example, in the United States, where the constitutional amendment process is complicated (requiring support by Congress and three-quarters of the states), changes to the Constitution have occasionally been reversed as occurred with Prohibition (the Eighteenth Amendment) which was rescinded in 1933 by a further amendment.

Another difference is that amendments to the Australian Constitution require a 'Yes' or 'No' vote and involve very specific changes to the wording of the Constitution. These changes are, of necessity, legal in nature, more difficult to understand, and have significant ramifications. It is quite unlike voting for a candidate and then hoping for the best. The legal aspects of a constitutional amendment might also mean that voters do not know what they are voting for at a referendum. For instance, in relation to the 1967 referendum concerning Aborigines, studies have shown that most voters thought they were giving Aborigines the vote. In fact, they voted to allow the Commonwealth government to be able to make laws for Aborigines – previously a State responsibility.

The first changes by referendum to the Australian Constitution took place in 1906, just five years after federation. Soon after, the notion arose that the public not only had to be alerted to the where, when and what about the referendum, as with elections, but also had to be 'informed' about the proposals and, therefore, the arguments for and against. This is quite different from expectations around elections.

The 1906 legislation for the first referendum, the *Referendum (Constitution Alteration) Act 1906-1910*, merely required the Chief Electoral Officer to ensure copies of the referendum proposal were sent to all States, be advertised and "to be exhibited at Post-Offices and Customs Houses ... and at such places as the Chief Electoral Officer directed...". The Act was concerned with promoting awareness of the proposed referendum vote rather than the merits or otherwise of the proposals.

This soon changed, spurred by the large number of referendum proposals that were being initiated during this period. The Fisher Labor Government made eight attempts to change the Constitution between 1911 and 1913. Amendments to the legislation were made in 1912 (following referenda in 1910) with passage of the *Referendum (Constitution Alteration) Act 1912*. This represented major change.

There was greater emphasis on providing information directly to voters that would include "an argument in favour" and "an argument against". These changes, which have remained in place, essentially enshrined the idea, the right, and the expectation that voters do have a choice and are free to vote 'Yes' or 'No'. More than that, there emerged an expectation that government has a role to play in ensuring voters are informed about both sides of the argument. There is nothing equivalent to this in the running of general elections.

While the Australian Electoral Commission (AEC) has functions concerning the veracity of information used in elections by candidates and parties, these functions are limited, hard to police, and do not extend to assessing different arguments about policies. That is something for the political players themselves who must debate one another and then persuade voters to make their own assessments. Perhaps the only time where there is some official and independent assessment of election issues by political opponents occurs when election promises are costed by Treasury and released to the public on the eve of the election.

Constitutional changes rules and processes

Changing the Australian Constitution is not simple. Unlike other countries constitutional change cannot be effected merely by whim either of the leader or of the legislature by just passing new legislation.

Section 128 of the Constitution sets out the basic rules. A referendum proposal must be embodied in a bill and then passed by parliament. The government then has two to six months to present the referendum to the people to vote on the proposal. It is to be voted on by all eligible voters. It requires a majority of voters, in a majority of States and a majority of voters across the whole nation for a referendum to be carried. This is known as a "double majority" requirement. It is much criticised by those who believe the Constitution should be more flexible. It is blamed for the failure of many referendums to pass – only eight out of forty-four attempts. The Labor Party, at one stage, wanted the Commonwealth Parliament alone, (which in effect would have meant the government alone), to be able to amend the Constitution simply by passing legislation in federal parliament.

These constitutional requirements are supplemented by legislation that sets out the processes of getting the referendum proposal, once decided by parliament, to the people so they can cast a vote. In a similar way, the *Commonwealth Electoral Act 1918* sets out arrangements for elections and the duties of the Australian Electoral Commission (AEC).

The first legislation pertaining to referendums, as mentioned, was the *Referendum (Constitution Alteration) Act 1906-10* passed to facilitate the first referendum (on Senate terms). It is now the *Referendum (Machinery Provisions) Act 1984* (Cth) which is amended from time to time, usually following a parliamentary committee report (the last such report was in December 2021). Governments are usually slow to act on these reports.

In summary, the process of holding a referendum involves the following stages:

- The Commonwealth government must initiate a referendum

by securing the passage of legislation through both houses of parliament;

- There must be a bill outlining the proposed amendment;
- There must be parliamentary debate about the bill (but this can be brief);
- Parliament must pass the bill;
- The referendum must be put to the people's vote between two to six months after the legislation is passed;
- Parliament decides the wording of the referendum question. Since the government is usually the sponsor of the referendum, wording is resolved by the government;
- Parliament decides the manner in which the referendum vote is taken;
- Voters must receive a pamphlet of the 'Yes' and 'No' case and these must be available to voters "not later than 14 days before" polling day;
- The 'Yes' and 'No' cases must be authorised by parliament. The referendum legislation sets down the rules about the wording of the referendum. The questions on the ballot paper must follow a prescribed format including the long title of the Bill for the referendum;
- In the event of no parliamentary opposition to a proposal, the practice has been for the voters to be presented with no 'No' case. This occurred with the 1967 Aboriginal referendum, the 1977 judge retirement amendment, and more recently would have occurred with the Rudd Government's proposed 2013 referendum on Commonwealth payments to local government; but that referendum did not proceed.
- If the government is supporting a 'Yes' case, as is usually the case, it will be responsible for the 'Yes' campaign whereas it will be left to the parliamentary opposition, or community groups, to mount and fund the 'No' case. The exception to this occurred in the 1999 republic referendum when the

Howard Government, which did not formally campaign for either case, provided funding to the 'Yes and 'No' campaign committees who were responsible for the campaigns;

- The AEC manages the voting processes, including where to vote, and promotion of awareness about the referendum as opposed to the specific content of the arguments

Implications

These processes and legislative provisions have implications for the forthcoming proposed referendum campaign on constitutional recognition.

Clearly, having a referendum involves presenting the electorate with the opportunity to decide 'Yes or 'No' on a particular issue. Voting 'No' is both expected and has long been practised. The fact that so few proposals have passed highlights the fact that voters often vote 'No', and do so by considerable margins. As Australia has a Westminster system, there is an official Opposition (an alternative government) whose role is to criticise the government, hold it to account, and to oppose, reject, or stymie a government's proposals by whatever legal and constitutional means possible. It is essentially an adversarial system in practice. However, there are many issues of concern about these arrangements that may militate against voters being able to cast a 'No' vote in an informed manner at a referendum.

First, it is up to the government to propose a referendum. It can decide its emphasis and title, which is what will go on the ballot paper. Moreover, in the early stages of resolving these issues, the government can appoint advisory committees and develop public consultation processes to develop the wording. As discussed, the government can do a considerable amount of pre-referendum campaigning. This is a common approach and has partly already been done in relation to the recognition issue; but it could be expanded further.

In effect, governments can set the agenda, co-opt supporters (and even opponents; after all, who can resist a call from the Prime Minister?), and build public support. Opponents are hard-pressed to get much air in this climate. Moreover, the lack of any agreed wording makes it hard to attack. The campaign has already begun, but it is largely one-sided.

Second, in preparing the 'Yes' case in the official documentation sent to voters, governments will naturally emphasise the positive, and downplay the negative.

Third, the government decides the timing of any legislation and thus the holding of any referendum. Its resources are vast and its timeframe flexible. It can choose the right time to maximise support for its proposals. It can delay passage of the actual legislation in order to continue campaigning on the issue.

Fourth, there is an issue relating to timing of the release of the official pamphlet containing details of the 'Yes' and 'No' cases. If it is only released, as required by legislation, no later than two weeks before the poll, it is too late. The direction and tone of the debate will have long been set.

Fifth, given the importance of parliament in deciding how arguments for and against are put, a question arises as to who is to compile the 'No' case; will there even be one? What if the Opposition decides to go along with the government - as is the Coalition's tendency on such issues? Isn't the current Opposition spokesman, Julian Leeser, in favour of the proposal? In that case who will mount the 'No' case? Will it be left to fringe parties like One Nation; and, if so, and how will that play out?

Sixth, there is the issue of other institutions in our government, like the States. Their opposition to referendum proposals in the past has often been a deciding factor leading to their defeat. After all, the States have resources and their premiers have high profiles. However, in this case there are no State interests at stake, at least not as yet. States will be either non-participative or supportive. This is also likely to be the case with our universities, churches, professional bodies, and most industry groups.

All this prompts the question as to who will actually represent the 'No' case and be recognised as such; or will presenting the 'No' view generate such opprobrium that no one will be willing to step forward? Indeed, will the 'No' campaign be given air at all?

Conclusion

Saying 'No' and opposing government ideas are long-accepted, cherished, and much practised parts of our system of government and liberal democracy. These practices are endemic to our Westminster system and apply to the day-to-day political wrangling between government and oppositions before, during, and after elections. This is the nature of all public debate in Australia – or at least used to be.

This characteristic of vigorous public debate has been further heightened in the last decade with the failure of successive federal governments to hold Senate majorities. They have had to deal with a recalcitrant cross bench comprising minority parties who often refuse to support the most basic changes being proposed.

Saying 'No' has been an essential feature of our referendum process, too. Although some have railed against the misinformation that has often been used to oppose certain referenda, it is hard to think how this can be overcome. It is an accepted part of the democratic political process. Opposing referenda by saying 'No' is seen as both normal and expected, whether driven by short-term politics or genuine concerns. Saying 'No' is also an important part of our culture covering interpersonal relations and in our exercise of individual choice in our daily lives. It is what liberals say they value most.

This chapter has argued that regardless of the arguments for and against the proposed referendum, the most important issue, the real test for our liberal democracy, is not so much the quality of the debate but whether there will be any debate at all. This is the issue that goes to the heart of the matter because what many people fear is that there will not be an open debate, and that those who oppose the proposal will be shunned where they work, ignored by the media, and sidelined in all sorts of ways.

How this referendum issue plays out in the next few months, or possibly years, will depend on many factors, such as our society's openness to debate, the stance of our political leaders and parties, and the attitude of the media and other institutions. It will also be influenced by existing laws and practices governing the running of federal constitutional referendums.

Most of all though, a successful referendum process depends on each of us having the freedom to exercise a right to say 'No' to a government proposal, and to be able to do so openly and freely in accordance with our beliefs. In recent times there has been too great a readiness to conform with the latest accepted conventional view, regardless of how it has emerged or what underpinned it.

There are, however, some to whom we can look to as an example as to how we might behave during the forthcoming referendum campaign.

We should start with our own H.V. (Bert) Evatt, who as leader of the federal Labor Parliamentary Party (1951-60), led a courageous 'No' campaign against the Menzies Government's referendum in 1951 to ban the Communist Party. Menzies had legitimate reasons for this proposal at the time as it was in the depths of the Cold War. It was a popular move too for a government struggling in office, but it raised real issues about freedom and choice. That is what Evatt saw as paramount. Some of his own party questioned Evatt's judgment; after all, he had just become leader following Ben Chifley's unexpected death and there was an expectation, based on opinion polls (73 percent), that the referendum would be successful. But Evatt told them he thought it "more important than a dozen elections".

Evatt held fast, campaigned early and vigorously, often by himself, and convincingly, and defeated the referendum. Menzies never had another referendum in his remaining nearly fifteen years as prime minister. Perhaps, as many now think, it was all for the best that Evatt won the day.

Suggested reading

Scott Bennett, *The Politics of Constitutional Amendment*, Research Paper No 11 2002-03, (Canberra: Commonwealth Parliamentary Library, 2003).

Brian Galligan, "Referendum", in Brian Galligan and Winsome Roberts, (eds.), *The Oxford Companion to Australian Politics*, (South Melbourne: Oxford University Press, 2007), pp. 498-500.

Matthew Lesh, *Democracy in a Divided Australia*, (Ballarat: Connor Court Publishing, 2018).

9

INDIGENOUS SOCIAL JUSTICE WON'T BE SOLVED WITH POETIC JUSTICE

Neenah Gray

Indigenous Australians are the only First Nations peoples that do not have a treaty in place with their national government; but does this mean Indigenous Australians are worse off than other Indigenous communities around the globe?

Similar social and political issues that exist within Australian Indigenous communities also persist in countries that have already signed constitutionally recognised agreements with their Indigenous peoples. These countries include New Zealand, which has the Waitangi Treaty signed in 1840, and Canada, which has a series of treaties with its Indigenous population. However, both New Zealand and Canada have repeatedly rejected Indigenous advice and gone against the treaties – particularly when there is a financial motive. Who can say that this will not be repeated in Australia?

Under Prime Minister Anthony Albanese, the Labor government elected in May 2022 is dedicated to upholding the Uluru Statement from the Heart as a constitutionally enshrined Indigenous voice to Parliament (see page ix). However, many people - both Indigenous and non-Indigenous – are confused as to how such a development could help to address the glaring social, health, and educational gaps that exist within Indigenous communities. The problem of over-generalised wording, combined with a dearth of information about the structure and proposed operation of the Voice, have left the Australian public confused as to how the Uluru Statement and Voice will help to overcome social disadvantage.

This chapter flags the dangerous tokenism occurring on social media that is targeting young people and major corporations. Both are arguably more concerned with a positive image of how they are seen in this debate than discussing the issue thoroughly. It will also compare the model for the Voice proposed by the Uluru Statement with the Waitangi Treaty and Tribunal in New Zealand, assessing the impact a legislated Voice has had on addressing the local government needs of Maori communities; and it will consider whether similar patterns might emerge in an Australian context.

Two of key phrases often heard to describe the Voice to Parliament are that it is to be "a road to self-determination" and "a call for truth-telling." Although these ideas sound fine in principle, they are simply repeated in advertising, academic papers, and social media in an attempt to explain the likely impact of the Uluru Statement and the Voice.

Despite the elaborate statements and ambiguous wording of the Uluru Statement, the approach to constitutional recognition is minimalist and limited with key members of the advisory group to be decided after the referendum. While the Voice to Parliament model proposed by the Uluru Statement is intended to ensure that local and regional Indigenous voices are heard, it would not have decision-making power; indeed, suggestions put forward by the advisory committee could be ignored altogether.

In this case, the Uluru Statement falls short of a treaty recognising sovereignty but sets up a structure founded on self-determination. Its purpose is not to create egalitarian justice; rather it would be to offer mutual acknowledgement that Australia was not *terra nullius*, and to assess the benefits accruing to all signatories. Arguably, the possibility of equitable distribution of opportunities that a treaty might bring about would be the result of greater Indigenous authority, together with opportunities to exercise influence and leadership in making public policy making. As the Indigenous Voice Fact Sheet states, the Uluru Statement and Voice to Parliament could "bring communities together" and could "advise the Australian Parliament and Government" on community-related issues, although some struggle is expected to overcome the tokenistic elements involved with these initiatives.

Indeed, symbolism and tokenism go hand in hand: the Uluru Statement from the Heart has taken on a tokenistic element on social media and within major corporations. Just as with the Closing the Gap initiative, the Uluru Statement has attracted plenty of business and corporate support. In 2020, more than 50 Indigenous organisations, as part of the Coalition of Peaks Indigenous organisation, signed an agreement to be included in Closing the Gap outcomes. According to the Coalition of Peaks, this has had a significant impact because it represents a new way of developing and implementing policy. Yet, time and again, the Closing the Gap initiatives have failed: the most recent data shows disappointing progress with just four of the seventeen targets on track to be met in the next decade.

While endorsement of the Uluru Statement by Australia's top corporations is strongly encouraged, such endorsement is only a symbolic and somewhat tokenistic gesture. For example, Fred Hollows Foundation suggests "10 Ways Your Business Can Support the Uluru Statement from the Heart" without being more specific than "sharing your support" and "donating". Suggestions six ("encourage your workplace to learn about cultural competency and its importance") and seven (implement workplace activities to encourage learning") are almost identical and display the same kind of tokenism.

Although intended to be motivational, all the suggestions are merely symbolic and lack proper direction. As such, actions prompted by the suggestions can be tokenistic and harmful, especially when a non-Indigenous person is interacting with matters of Indigenous culture. As law professor, Megan Davis, has remarked, "If you look at the trajectory of Aboriginal advocacy for structural change, the kind that actually will make a big difference, every time we get close to it, we just choose to do really inane things as a nation that don't get us anywhere but make everyone feel good."

Furthermore, social media displays troubling tokenism in its effort to create 'movements' for a 'better cause'. An example of this occurred in the 'Black Lives Matter' (BLM) campaign in 2020 when, on one day, many people posted a black square to black out Instagram in the hope of addressing police brutality in the USA. Nothing was offered by way of explaining either the black square or the objectives of BLM: those who logged onto Instagram that day were simply met with a parade of black squares which provoked a guilty conscience and the need to appease their followers to stay woke.

Blanket statements can be generated on social media platforms, such as Instagram, without offering any explanation about objectives. The Uluru Statement from the Heart has taken to Instagram, sharing positive posts but offering little or no information, and many non-Indigenous people simply jump reflexively on the bandwagon without without even bothering to ask what members of Indigenous communities truly might think of the initiative, or if there are better ideas. People such as this can be thought of as 'tokenists', and they can be found throughout the crowds of Uluru Statement supporters.

There are many 'infographics' on Instagram that purport to explain any number of causes, from 'Defunding the Police' to 'Ways You Can Help Besides Posting on Instagram'. While it might seem a good idea to promote political ideas and social movements on social media, particularly Instagram, doing so often displays a dangerous tokenism devoid of the education needed in order to engage meaningfully in issues such as enshrining an Indigenous voice to parliament. Indigenous people that oppose the Uluru Statement are on a collision course with tokenists as we approach this referendum.

As the landscape of Indigenous political and social affairs changes, so do the notions of symbolism, arguably to the point where they can be harmful and tokenistic. What could be more catchy than a heart emoji in support of the Uluru Statement? Charles Jacobs has argued that the uncertain protocols surrounding many symbolic acts leave room for tokenism to occur, especially coming from a non-Indigenous person interacting with Indigenous affairs.

The danger of yielding to symbolism and tokenism in addressing Indigenous political and social issues is that nothing actually gets addressed at all, least of the pressing economic, educational and social issues facing Indigenous communities.

Equivalent systems of cultural and constitutional recognition in different countries, most notably New Zealand, present a clear idea of the limitations and tokenism still present, with little change to the overall social outcomes of their Indigenous population.

As mentioned previously, the Uluru Statement's Indigenous Voice to Parliament will not enjoy any official power or exercise any decision-making authority over Indigenous issues. Suggestions made by the established body could therefore be ignored. This has happened in New Zealand where the Waitangi Tribunal was established in 1975 to ensure that the measures and protocols of the Waitangi Treaty were being upheld. Despite having a reputation for its progressive legislative system, New Zealand's Maori population still remains under-represented and lacks meaningful opportunities to engage in local government authority decision making.

Steps have been taken to improve Maori representation in local government, such as provision made in the *Local Electoral Act 2001* for establishing Maori wards or constituencies. However, only one regional council, the Waikato Regional Council, has so far established Maori constituencies in its district, when two Maori seats were created before the 2013 elections. All this in a country which enjoys the Waitangi Treaty and the Waitangi Tribunal, and has many Maori members serving in parliament.

A challenge for the Uluru Statement from the Heart and the Indigenous Voice to Parliament is to ensure there is as much community engagement – as possible.

To date, there is no consensus in the Aboriginal and Torres Strait Islander Community that the Uluru Statement from the Heart is the path to realise self-determination. At best the Uluru Statement is a product of the Recognise campaign coopted by an Indigenous elite to achieve all things for all Australian people voting at a referendum. Many of those who desired a Treaty foremost walked out of the process, frustrated by a lack of discussion that was framed by the limited objective of constitutional recognition. At the time, then PM Malcolm Turnbull disregarded the Referendum Council's Uluru Statement for going beyond its terms of reference, and not being representative enough of the Indigenous Community.

Unfortunately the 272 pages of the Tom Calma and Marcia Langton 2021 Co-Design Final Report did not go much further and only outlines a process of establishing 30-35 local and regional voices that feed into the National Voice to speak for the 300 Aboriginal and Torres Strait Islander countries in Australia. This is sparse compared to the settlement between the Noongar people and the West Australian Government that has been hailed as Australia's first Treaty. The Noongar People have no less than 7 local and regional voices for their 30,000 people.

As can been seen in New Zealand, there may be many stumbling blocks along the way before realising the structural change. New Zealand has much to teach Australia before we enshrine an Indigenous Voice to Parliament in this country. For despite having an enshrined voice in legislation and parliament, Maori people still face some of the same social problems that exist in Australia.

In Australia, Indigenous people contribute to more than 29 percent of the overall prison system, despite making up less than 3 percent of the general population. A report from 2018 by the New Zealand Department of Corrections found that 50 percent of their prisoners were Maori, compared to 40 percent recorded in 1971, even though Maori people only comprise up 16 percent of New Zealand's population. In regard to land rights issues, governments of New Zealand have repeatedly rejected the Waitangi Tribunal's recommendations that Maori people be given sea rights over foreshore and seabeds for hunting and continuation of cultural practices.

This is somewhat reflected in the recognition of Land Rights and Native Title in Australia, where cases are repeatedly rejected before any official claim is formalised. It remains a real concern for Indigenous and non-Indigenous Australians that over time the Uluru Statement and the Voice will become merely a symbolic gesture that has leveraged unceded sovereignty while leaving pressing social problems unresolved.

Some believe that Australia should focus on treaty making before establishing an Indigenous Voice to Parliament. Others acknowledge that there are record numbers of Indigenous people in Australian Parliament and this will be the turning point to bring structural change as a nation.

Senator Jacinta Nampijinpa Price argues that unity of both Indigenous and non-Indigenous Australians will be the foundation of moving forward as a nation and delivering practical outcomes to Indigenous communities. Senator Price has previously mentioned that some Indigenous communities do not agree with the Uluru Statement, making the process of establishing an Indigenous Voice potentially even more difficult than proposed. Certain things need to be perfected before establishing the Uluru Statement as an official foundation to an Indigenous Voice to Parliament.

In conclusion, the Uluru Statement from the Heart has demonstrated that there are significant problems to be addressed before proper implementation of an initiative such as an Indigenous Voice. Tokenism has become a major feature of the way the Uluru Statement has been interpreted by major Australian corporations and young people on social media; there is genuine concern that the Uluru Statement and an Indigenous Voice will become a merely symbolic gesture.

As Australia prepares to take on the responsibilities of an enshrined Voice to Parliament, there is much to be thought through with care before voting 'yes' in the referendum to enact legislation. The road to strengthening Indigenous voices in parliament is a long one, and no shortcuts should be taken.

Suggested reading

Jordan Humphreys, "A voice to parliament will do little for Indigenous justice", *Redflag*, (25 June 2022).

Dominic O'Sullivan, "Treaties and re-setting the colonial relationship: Lessons for Australia from the Treaty of Waitangi", *Ethnicities*, 2021, 21(6), 1070-1092.

Charles Jacobs, "Symbolism and substance in Indigenous Affairs", *Policy*, Vol.33, No.4, (2017-2018).

10

THE VOICE: WHAT ARE WE BEING ASKED TO DECIDE?

Caroline Di Russo

I am someone who is always willing to be convinced. I am not so schooled or set in my views on the topic of constitutional recognition that I cannot be swayed by a compelling argument either way. On a first principles basis, I simply start here: all citizens should be treated equally under the law; and they ought to have the same rights, responsibilities, and enfranchisement.

To that end, I need to be convinced why one race should have its own 'voice' under the Australian Constitution. Why should one group of citizens be treated differently to any other group on the basis of race? I have not yet been given a compelling reason why the existing flaws in the development and implementation of Indigenous-related policy can't be fixed under the current system, or a new Voice enshrined in the Constitution will provide better outcomes for Indigenous Australians.

My parents and grandparents were post-war migrants to Australia and I am the first generation to have been born here. Therefore, I approach the discussion about constitutional recognition without any of the cultural or generational baggage some in this country seem to have, as though they carry the guilt of generations past. I approach the matter with an open mind.

As much as some would have us believe otherwise, this decision cannot be an emotional one. It must be rational. Clear-headed. Analytical. We should aim for mature and robust debate on this issue and encourage voters to make their own informed decisions. Whenever the electorate is asked to change the Constitution, it potentially sets Australia on a course that will reverberate for decades. It is much more than political posturing for the current parliamentary term.

So, I'm not here to tell you what to think; I simply encourage you to think for yourself. To have an open and inquiring mind. To form your own view after analysing the information before you. And to vote accordingly. Being able to make an informed decision requires voters to be provided with sufficient information about what they are voting for and why they are voting for it.

In this case, there is scant detail about the proposal to enshrine a Voice to Parliament in the Constitution. We do not know what this Indigenous advisory body will look like, who will represent who, or what its remit will be. It is said that this body will not have a power of veto, it will not be a third chamber, and its advice will not be justiciable. But what the Voice *will* be is as important for the electorate to know as what it won't be.

In the advertising world, there is much talk about how to convert a consideration into a purchase. And while this doesn't sit perfectly flush with the notion of constitutional change, it does help us understand how people make decisions and what level of information they require to get on board. Whether it is about consumer goods or constitutional change, people need to be given a reason to take a positive step. It removes doubt and motivates people to make a choice.

Where is the detail?

In an interview, the Minister for Indigenous Australians, Linda Burney, said she did not want the referendum question to get bogged down in what the Voice would look like. Rather, she wanted the Australian population simply to decide whether or not they wanted the Voice. Referring to the 1999 republic referendum, Burney said the problem was "that instead of the question being 'Should Australia be a Republic', it became about the model." The simplicity of the question was lost, Burney said, and the Australian public voted 'no'. The debate in 1999 was around the model, not whether or not we should be a Republic. Burney does not want the same fate to occur in this referendum. "It's really important that the question be about whether there should be a Voice," she said, "not about what sort of Voice it will be."

The Republic referendum did provide a model for the proposed republic but it was principally a debate between Constitutional Monarchists and Republicans. The main debate was not between two schools of Republicans. Yes, there was plenty of discussion around the model, but there were also a great many people who did not see the benefit in trying to fix a system that was not broken; or they voted against choosing a system they thought was, on balance, inferior to the one we currently have.

Reform must be perceived as being a net-benefit if people are to be induced to vote in favour of it. And in order to determine whether it's going to be a net-benefit, voters need sufficient information to appreciate its strengths and deficiencies.

It is unhelpful to compare the proposed constitutional recognition referendum to the Republic referendum. Indeed, the comparison threatens to doom it. Rather than encouraging us to weigh constitutional recognition on its own merits, it encourages us to look at it through the prism of a failed past referendum which was concerned with a very different question. After all, the debate about whether or not to enshrine an Indigenous advisory body in the Constitution is very different from one about substituting one complete system of government for another.

The difficulty I have with the position taken by Burney is that she expects people to vote for the Voice to Parliament without explaining what the Voice is and how it would fit into our current system of government.

While there are different models around the world for a republic, there are far fewer models for a constitutionally enshrined Voice to Parliament. Indeed, there are no well-known examples to help voters understand and appreciate the type of advisory body they are being asked to vote in favour of. To give the Voice any chance of success, the Albanese Government must give the voting public a clear understanding of the fundamental structure of the Voice and the bounds of its jurisdiction.

Mark Leibler, co-chair of both the Expert Panel and the Referendum Council on Constitutional Recognition of Aboriginal and Torres Strait Islander Australians, has remarked that "development of a more detailed model would lead to only one eventuality – a devastating No vote. Those who argue otherwise are, consciously or unconsciously, motivated by a desire to sabotage the process." Although this sounds to me a little like a blame-shifting narrative in case the referendum is not successful, surely, it is controversial to suggest that any person who asks for detail on the Voice is trying to sabotage the process. We should encourage voters to be informed; to have an open, mature, and substantive discussion about what the Voice to Parliament is designed to achieve; and to vote dispassionately, rather than gaslight them into submission simply because they want to know about what they are voting for.

Of equal importance is a broad discussion of the 'no' position. The views of those opposed to enshrining the Voice should have an equal platform to those in favour. And while there are many Indigenous advocates for the Voice, there are also Indigenous advocates who oppose it. Their views must not be dismissed out of hand simply because they do not suit the prevailing fashion. If we want to give Indigenous people a Voice, we should respect all Indigenous voices, not just those deemed to be on 'the right side of history'. Ultimately, without sufficient detail, the capability of either side to mount a compelling case is limited. And that is not how divisions are mended or gaps closed.

The proposed wording

In 2021, the National Indigenous Australians Agency released its final report to the Australian Government. The report, the *Indigenous Voice Co-Design Process*, provides detail about the proposed design of the Voice and how it would function. This report would be a good starting point for a discussion about constitutional recognition. However, at the 2022 Garma Festival, Prime Minister Anthony Albanese skirted around accepting the model in the Co-Design Process as the one upon which the Voice would be based. Instead, he said there would be further consultation after the referendum. Sadly, this sort of obfuscation does little to fill the information gap and instead creates further uncertainty about what the Voice would actually look like.

It was at the same Garma festival that the Prime Minister released the proposed wording for the referendum:

- There shall be a body, to be called the Aboriginal and Torres Strait Islander Voice.
- The Aboriginal and Torres Strait Islander Voice may make representations to Parliament and the Executive government on matters relating to Aboriginal and Torres Strait Islander Peoples.
- The Parliament shall, subject to this Constitution, have power to make laws with respect to the composition, functions, powers and procedures of the Aboriginal and Torres Strait Islander Voice.

He also proposed the following "simple" question as the one to put to the Australian people:

Do you support an alteration to the Constitution that establishes an Aboriginal and Torres Strait Islander Voice?

Perhaps the question is too simple. In fact, it looks very much as if the proposed constitutional change would give any government *carte blanche* to make the Voice much more than an advisory body. While parading as a simple model, lack of detail about the Voice means the enshrined advisory body could be given any powers or functions that the Parliament decides, subject, of course, to the remainder of the Constitution.

Unable to analyse the potential scope of the Voice, or to decide whether it adds to, or detracts from, the Constitution and the progress of Indigenous affairs, those who support an advisory Voice in principle might be dissuaded.

As expected, the proposed wording of the referendum

was reported extensively in the media. What was slightly unexpected was the broad concern, across mastheads, about the need for additional detail without which, it was feared, the referendum would be doomed to fail.

The *Sydney Morning Herald* and the *Age*, and by extension their readership, tend towards being sympathetic towards the progressive view of the world, and so the comments attached to their reporting were particularly instructive. Specifically, there were numerous comments by those who supported the Voice in principle but who still wanted an appreciation of what they were actually voting for before voting for it. Also noticeable was a healthy scepticism from those who were not interested in voting in favour of a 'just trust us' referendum question.

This should set alarm bells ringing for the Federal Government. And no matter how often the government uses the word "simple", this does not make up for the evident deficiency of the proposal. I am not suggesting reams of detail about the minutia are necessary but rather that the basic structure, functions, and limitations of jurisdiction need to be evident so that the Parliament, and by extension the High Court, have a clear understanding of what the Voice can and cannot do.

The current proposed wording to be inserted into the Constitution makes no express provision that the Voice be solely an advisory body. Instead, the Parliament is to be given an unfettered power to create any sort of body it sees fit insofar as it relates to powers, functions, composition, and procedures. The only express restriction is that the Voice is subject to the Constitution. The paragraph relating to the powers and functions is also not substantively limited by the preceding paragraph; the preceding paragraph only states that the Voice 'may make' representations to Parliament but it does not otherwise expressly limit the capability of the Voice.

This lack of clarity is likely to cause doubt and confusion because while there may be broad support for an advisory body, there is unlikely to be the same level of support for a body which has powers or jurisdiction in excess of that. The preference should be for the jurisdiction of the Voice to be expressed in the Constitution much like the jurisdiction of the Courts or the legislative powers of the Federal Parliament.

And this is the material point: even those who support a Voice in principle may be wary of supporting a form of the Voice which they consider to be deficient in detail or which can gain a life of its own beyond what voters thought they were voting for. Additionally, those who are currently unconvinced are likely to remain unconvinced as the deficiency in the drafting reaffirms their doubts.

What do we want to achieve?

The purpose of the Voice is to create an advisory body to provide a voice to over 200 different indigenous groups situated over the entire expanse of Australia so that there can be better input to policy to produce better outcomes of Indigenous people. Though I sense we are having the conversation in the wrong order.

We should be talking about what outcomes we want to achieve for Indigenous Australians across the country and what structure will help Australia best achieve those ends. There is no benefit in creating a burgeoning bureaucracy if it does not improve living, education, and economic standards for Indigenous Australians. We have seen so many bodies, structures, and projects designed to improve the lives of

Indigenous Australians that have failed miserably in achieving that outcome. This is one area where there have been too few positive results despite major investment. It isn't that Australians are unhappy to spend the money; the issue is that the outcomes which are produced are clearly not reflective of the level of funding.

A change to the Constitution is a serious matter; how this change will improve the lives and circumstances of Indigenous Australians will be front of mind for all Australians. It is incumbent on those who promote the Voice to explain why the Voice is likely to achieve better results than the Indigenous bodies, structures, and bureaucracies that have gone before.

Why make a change unless it is going to fix the issue that underpins the proposal? There is a material risk that a Voice could be enshrined into the Constitution that may not achieve what it is meant to achieve; or worse, further disenfranchise or disadvantage Indigenous Australians as their voice is stifled below yet another layer of bureaucracy.

Burney wishes to see the Voice enshrined in the Constitution so that "it cannot be arbitrarily dismissed by any government" compared to previous incarnations of indigenous advisory bodies that have been disbanded over the years. But this does not deal squarely with the substance of the issue. Previous incarnations of Indigenous advisory bodies were not disbanded for mere political convenience; they were disbanded because they were expensive, dysfunctional and failed to provide better outcomes for Indigenous Australians.

We all want to see better outcomes for Indigenous Australians, but it is doubtful a shiny new version of ATSIC, which cannot be dismantled if it is ineffective, is the way to achieve those outcomes.

Indigenous questioning of the Voice

There are obviously some Indigenous Australians who will oppose the Voice outright. That is their right. The notion that all Indigenous Australians want the Voice, or are monolithic in their thinking, is wrong and, frankly, infantilising. Some of them have written contributions to this book, and so I urge you to read their views firsthand. Unsurprisingly, there has also been opposition to this detail-lite approach from well-respected indigenous advocates and public policy specialists, including Pat Turner and Noel Pearson.

Turner has had decades of involvement in Indigenous policy and knows it strengths and limitations intimately. She believes education opportunities and outcomes for Indigenous children are just as important as a Voice to Parliament but is frustrated that the former doesn't receive the same attention as the latter. We would do well to consider her concerns. We would also do well to query whether the latter would improve the former.

At a recent Australian-Israeli Chamber of Commerce event in June 2022, she noted that that Aboriginal and Torres Strait Islander people had unanswered questions, and made the following observations:

> This is a deeply personal view. I am struggling to see the best way forward on constitutional recognition and responding to the Uluru Statement. I accept the totality of the Uluru Statement and I am very supportive of a national voice to the parliament, but I need to start to see some detail here. I want some meat on the bones. And the proponents of the voice have got to start putting that out because I am not the only Aboriginal person that is wondering what this is going to look like.

Her views are entirely reasonable and reflect concerns of Indigenous and non-Indigenous Australians alike. And given her deep and long-standing involvement in Indigenous related public policy, no doubt the detail would allow her to determine whether, based on her experience, she considers that the Voice would improve outcomes for Indigenous Australians where previous attempts have failed.

Similarly, Noel Pearson, a passionate supporter of the Voice, summed it up beautifully when he said, "Australians, and parliament itself, would want to see what the body looks like, and hear what the voice sounds like, before they vote on it". He is also on the record saying:

> We're going to design all of the detail, present it to the Australian people and the parliament and say, this is what we're talking about in terms of how the voice would operate, what it would do and so on. And that has to be done prior to the conduct of a referendum.

Again, this is an entirely reasonable approach. And both these voices need to be given room alongside the advocates in favour of the Voice proposal as it is. Their views are equally valid and worthy of our consideration.

Conclusion

I am yet to form a firm view on the Voice to Parliament but I need more than the information before me to form that view. When it comes to changing our Constitution, it is not appropriate to make superficial, rash, and emotional decisions. Constitutional change should be dispassionate, objective, and purposeful – otherwise we can end up creating more issues, both legal and cultural, than we hope to solve. We also risk creating bigger divisions than those we are trying to bridge.

We do not need every last detail; but we do need sufficient information to inform our decision-making. We need more than a single, thin, incontestable narrative. To the government: help us help you.

11

CONSTITUTIONAL RECOGNITION IS NOT NECESSARY FOR INTEGRATION – AUSTRALIA'S MIGRANT STORY TELLS US SO

Rocco Loiacono

There is no truer saying, it seems, than 'History repeats itself'. In 1988, the debate surrounding Aboriginal land rights received about the same level of attention that the debate on a constitutionally enshrined Aboriginal and Torres Strait Islander 'Voice' to Parliament is presently. The then Prime Minister Bob Hawke was supportive of land rights and, when Parliament met for the first time in the new Parliament House on May 9 of that year, he supported a resolution that Indigenous Australians had been dispossessed of their land. A few years previously, Hawke had planned to introduce land rights legislation but encountered strong opposition from within his own party, notably from Western Australia and its then Premier, Brian Burke.

Further, Aboriginal land rights did not have the backing of those on the conservative side of politics at the time. As recounted by the late David Barnett in *John Howard, Prime Minister* (Penguin, 1997), the above-mentioned resolution, and the notion of land rights, were opposed by then Opposition

Leader John Howard. In words that now seem prophetic, Howard declared: "I do not accept the doctrine of hereditary guilt." He explained that yes, in the past, wrongs were done to Aboriginals, but they weren't done by him, or his parents, or indeed his generation. Howard stated, tellingly: "We are a separate, distinct, Australian nation, of which Aboriginals are a part, an honoured part, a special part, and I am all in favour of giving them special help. They need it." He concluded with these words: "I am strongly against dividing the country between black and white. I think that is a recipe for disaster."

Howard consistently held this position in public life, notably while in office as prime minister from 1996 to 2007. He repeatedly cautioned against depicting Australia's history since 1788 as little more than a disgraceful record of imperialism, exploitation and racism. He wrote in his autobiography, *Lazarus Rising* (Harper Collins, 2010, page 277) that:

> Such a portrayal is a gross distortion and deliberately neglects the overall story of great Australian achievement that there is in our history to be told, and such an approach will be repudiated by the overwhelming majority of Australians who are proud of what this country has achieved although inevitably acknowledging the blemishes of its past history.

Like the history of any country, Australia's has its blemishes, not limited to the treatment of Indigenous people. As the son of migrants, I know first-hand the injustices and hardships my parents and grandparents suffered when they decided to come to a country on the other side of the world, with a completely different language and culture, to try and make a life for themselves and escape a Europe which, even though being rebuilt, still bore many scars, both psychological and economic, from the horrors of war.

In a piece in the *Spectator Australia* on June 30, 2022, Marc

Hendrickx advocated for the so-called 'Third Wave' of migrants to gain their own 'voice' to Parliament and be recognised in the Constitution. He suggested that there be an *Australis Statement from the Sea*, named after the ship *Australis* that brought many migrants to Australia, as a call for recognition. He wrote:

> We are the many Wogs, Krauts, Frogs, Czechs, Poles, Chings, Curry munchers, Poms, and other migrants who arrived here since the end of the Great War. Many suffered abuse for their strange cultural practices, their odd surnames, and accents, taste in food and clothing, and ignorance of the bush and the beach.

Hendrickx added, significantly: "There has never been an apology to these hard-working families for the abuse they suffered as they dropped their own cultural practises and assimilated into modern Australia. They get no recognition in our founding document."

In his piece, Hendrickx also called for "truth-telling about our shared past as the basis for lasting reconciliation."

Now, obviously much of this is satirical, but beneath that veneer there is a serious question to be answered here and it resonates with me, as a son of this Third Wave. It recognises that there were some blemishes in Australia's past treatment of migrants; but does this mean Third Wave migrants and their descendants need a distinct 'voice' for them as a basis for ensuring their integration into Australian society and lasting reconciliation based on the wrongs of the past?

The history of migration to this country has demonstrated, without any doubt, that the answer to this question is a resounding 'no'. Those of the Third Wave, and their sons and daughters, despite prejudice and numerous setbacks, integrated successfully into Australian society without the need for any constitutionally enshrined 'voice' to help them do so. To this end, there are episodes I can recount from my family's experience as migrants in Western Australia in the late 1950s, and, in the hope you will forgive me this indulgence, I will briefly focus on a couple, in particular.

The first was when my mother, at eight years of age, contracted rheumatic fever and was subsequently hospitalised not long after she and my grandparents arrived in Australia. My grandfather was employed, as many migrant men were, to clear bush near Balingup in the south-west of Western Australia, so the local hospital was at least seven miles away, probably more. Out in the bush, they couldn't afford a car – an asset still out of reach of most Australians in those days, let alone newly arrived migrants – and any bus service (if there even was one) was intermittent and unreliable. So, the only way to get to the hospital was to walk; and that is what my grandmother did, every day, heavily pregnant at the time, only to be told by the matron, upon finally arriving at the hospital, that she could not see her own daughter because she arrived outside visiting hours. So, naturally distraught, my grandmother was forced to walk those miles home. This went on for weeks.

The second episode occurred a little later on when my grandparents managed, in partnership with siblings, to invest and work in a dairy farm. It wasn't long before their house burned down and they had to start over. Is it any wonder that about half of all Italians who came to Australia went back? Hardships and setbacks such as these, the harshness of the terrain and the climate, the strangeness and hostility of some sectors of a country which was at the time, despite official government policies, less than welcoming, meant the nostalgia for the old country proved to be too much.

As it turned out, my family was part of the 50 per cent that stayed. They moved to Perth and ended up establishing and running successful family businesses. They integrated well into Australia, and did so without any collective guilt. Let's face it, southern Italy is a far more scarred part of the world – even a cursory glance at the last 2500 years of the history of the region will tell you that. But my family integrated in Australia without any kind of affirmative action; they were spared paternalistic attitudes that they had to be helped because they were considered as being marginalised or disadvantaged; and they definitely did not benefit from any kind of bureaucratic or parliamentary, let alone constitutional, intervention.

The story of my family is just one of many stories of migrants overcoming adversity, and many are far more harrowing. Several are recounted by Susanna Iuliano in her work, *Vite Italiane: Italian lives in Western Australia* (UWA Publishing, 2010). There are two periods in particular that I would like to focus on: first, anti-Italian sentiment on the WA Goldfields between the two World Wars; and second, the internment of Italians during World War II.

Anti-Italian riots

Iuliano describes various incidents in her book of anti-European, and in particular, anti-Italian, sentiment in Kalgoorlie and Boulder, affecting the lives and livelihoods of these migrants. In 1916, Greek migrants became the targets of drunken rioters, many of whom were returned servicemen. The rioters were inflamed by an editorial in the *Kalgoorlie Miner* newspaper blaming the King of Greece for allied casualties in Athens, and rioters ransacked and looted businesses and properties in the two towns.

As Iuliano's research reveals, in 1919 and 1934, rioters' attention turned more specifically to Italians, who comprised the vast majority of the mining workforce.

The first specific episodes Iuliano recounts refer to rioting in 1919 after the stabbing of a returned serviceman, Thomas Northwood, by an Italian migrant, Giacomo 'James' Gotti. The trouble began when the drunken Northwood called Gotti and a party of Italian friends, including women, "Dago bastards" outside the Café Majestic on Hannan Street, Kalgoorlie's main street. Blows were then exchanged and, in retaliation, Gotti went and got a carving knife from the café kitchen and stabbed Northwood, who died from his wounds two days later.

Following this, the local RSL branch called for the closure of all Italian businesses and the deportation of all Italian males from the Goldfields. After the meeting, drunken mobs went through the town, attacking Italian businesses, and many Italians fled. Once the situation was brought under control, Gotti was charged with wilful murder and prosecuted. However, claims for compensation by the Italian consul on behalf of those who lost their livelihoods were dismissed by the WA government.

The second riot, in 1934, occurred after another drunken episode, when local miner and sportsman Edward Jordan was evicted from the Home from Home Hotel on Hannan Street by its proprietor, Claudio 'Charlie' Mattaboni. A scuffle ensued and Mattaboni punched Jordan, who fell and hit his head on the kerb, dying several hours later in hospital. The spectre of the 1919 riots was raised when underlying economic, social, and racial prejudices against Italians came to the fore and mobs ransacked, looted, and burned Italian-owned businesses in Kalgoorlie and Boulder.

Many miners then went on strike and attacked the makeshift shacks in which the Italians lived on Dingbat Flat in Boulder. The 'Battle of Dingbat Flat' claimed two lives and resulted in further destruction of property. In the newspapers of the time, politicians and editors condemned the rioters in the strongest possible terms, noting that the "great majority of foreigners are hard-working, decent and honest and have accepted Australian citizenship. Their children will be Australian born and bred, and thousands of present native-born Australians are not ashamed of such parentage."

The accounts of the Italians at the time of the riots note animosity born out of jealousy of wealthy Italian businesses on the Goldfields. Indeed, as Iuliano notes, most of the charges laid by police were for destruction of property and possession of stolen goods. While many Italians left Kalgoorlie and started afresh elsewhere, many believed that no matter how successful or integrated they were, they did not 'belong'.

Second World War internment

When Italy entered the war in June 1940 on the side of the Axis powers, Italians were classified as 'enemy aliens' and a significant proportion were interned. In Western Australia itself, around 1200 Italians were interned in prisons and camps in Fremantle, Rottnest, Harvey, Kalgoorlie and in Loveday Internment Camp in South Australia. Under the Commonwealth *National Security Act 1939*, the army working with local police could detain anyone "reasonably suspected of being likely to act in a manner prejudicial to the public safety or defence of the Commonwealth." As Iuliano outlines, such broad and vaguely defined powers made it more likely that racial and economic prejudices would influence the decisions and actions of the army commanders and state police who compiled the lists of internees.

It did not matter that many internees were already naturalised

Australians with successful businesses. What is more, many internees had sons and brothers serving in the Australian armed forces. Several were not released until many months after Italy signed the armistice on 8 September 1943 and declared war on Germany. While obviously causing a sense of dislocation and distrust in these internees, upon their release, most did their best to resume their activities and 'keep their head down'.

In 1991, at a dinner at state Parliament House in Perth, then prime minister Bob Hawke acknowledged that internment was a mistake influenced more by the anti-immigrant attitudes of the time than by any real threat to national security:

> Experiences such as yours, as internees, strengthened by the good will which you have consistently shown to a nation that was at the time much less welcoming, have helped Australians develop a much more mature and sophisticated attitude to our multicultural society.

The same can be said for all migrants who have come to Australia, in particular those who came following World War II. Yet in spite of the tumult and disruption experienced in the past, we do not hear calls, either from the migrants themselves, or from their descendants, for a 'voice' to make right past injustices. Indeed, as I have argued, no such thing was needed to achieve integration or reconciliation.

Heads of religious denominations have declared their public support for a constitutionally-enshrined Indigenous 'Voice' to the Commonwealth Parliament, as have several on the conservative side of politics. These include Greg Craven, former Vice-Chancellor of the Australian Catholic University and constitutional law scholar, and Mark Leibler, senior partner at Arnold Bloch Leibler, and co-chair of both the Expert Panel and the Referendum Council on Constitutional Recognition of Aboriginal and Torres Strait Islander Australians.

I respect both Craven and Leibler. However, even though I acknowledge the sincerity of their arguments, I cannot get past the view that, when one steps back, the 'Voice' is still, deep down, motivated by a sense of guilt and the need to atone in some way for the wrongs of the past.

Migrants and Aboriginal Australians were at times brutally mistreated in our history and many have suffered continuing disadvantage. However, that is not a justification for breaching the principle that all people are equal not only in the eyes of the law, but also, and probably more importantly, in fundamental status.

The fact of the matter is that *E pluribus unum* is a reality in this country across all parliaments in Australia and reflects Australia's success as a nation of migrants. Our current prime minister, Anthony Albanese, is of Italian heritage. The Minister for Industry and Science, Ed Husic, was the first Muslim to be elected to the Commonwealth Parliament and the first Muslim to be made a minister in the federal government. The Morrison government had Michael Sukkar, of Lebanese heritage, and Zed Seselja, of Croatian heritage, as ministers. Joe Hockey, of part Armenian heritage, was a senior minister in the Howard and Abbott governments. Both sides of politics in New South Wales have produced premiers and ministers of migrant heritage, which is also the case in every other state.

It's not just migrants who have flourished. Since Neville Bonner was elected to represent Queensland in the Senate, both sides of politics, at both state and Commonwealth level, have a proud record of electing Indigenous Australians as parliamentarians.

Senator Bonner's legacy was the appointment of his grandniece, Joanna Lindgren, to fill a Queensland Senate casual vacancy from 2015 until 2016. In 2010, Ken Wyatt became the first Indigenous Australian to be elected to the House of Representatives, and in 2019 he was appointed as a Minister in Cabinet. Two more Indigenous Coalition members of the Senate, Senators Jacinta Nampijinpa Price (Country Liberal NT) and Kerrynne Liddle (Liberal SA) were elected in 2022.

Senator Jacinta Price has observed that the Voice is based on an advisory body set up in the Northern Territory some 20 years ago; but, she asks, is it merely a tokenistic gesture that will have no real practical solutions for Indigenous Australians?

Writing in the *Spectator Australia* on July 14, 2022, Stephen Fryson wondered whether the existence of the 'Voice' is going to address the challenges of domestic violence, sexual abuse, and poverty cycles which occur within too many of our remote Aboriginal communities. Will it improve declining literacy levels for children and adults? Fryson is not alone: this is a point made eloquently and repeatedly by Senator Price, who highlighted that many Indigenous Australians living in remote communities, similarly to migrants, do not have a command of English as their first language.

Moreover, as Price has also stated, one cannot escape the threat that a constitutionally enshrined 'Voice' will actually serve to divide Australians on the grounds of ethnicity. It also appears to assume that simply because someone is Indigenous, that person is automatically marginalised. Unfortunately, many members of our society are marginalised.

My own family, as well as communities of migrants who lost their lives or had their livelihoods destroyed in Kalgoorlie, experienced miserable feelings of not belonging. But those communities were not overwhelmed by affirmative action-type policies or official government statements that they represented a marginalised group; rather, adversity was overcome by means of practical measures and a recognition that hard work, not a hand out, was the recipe for success.

We now risk a revival of the 'us' and 'them' mentality which helped to fuel the animosity directed towards migrants. As John Howard warned all those years ago, dividing the country into black and white will be a disaster for a house divided against itself cannot stand. Howard's successors in the Liberal Party could do worse than heed his prophetic words.

For all these reasons, I remain unconvinced that the 'Voice' can be, as Greg Craven hopes, "something that will make us, as a people and Australia as a nation, truly better". I do not question Craven's sincerity which, no doubt, is driven by his faith, given his appeal, in arguing for a 'Voice', on the dignity of the human person.

However, St Paul's words in his Letter to the Galatians, the ultimate Christian statement of the inherent dignity of each person, ring true for me: "There is neither Jew nor Gentile, neither slave nor free, nor is there male and female, given you are all one in Christ Jesus" (3:28). This inherent dignity means that every human being is endowed equally with rights and obligations. It is the sentiment that motivated the American Declaration of Independence and its most famous statement:

> We hold these truths to be self-evident, that all men are created equal, that they are endowed by their Creator with certain unalienable Rights, that among these are Life, Liberty and the pursuit of Happiness.

Implementing this ideal over the last two centuries has been the great calling of the Western liberal democratic tradition. The state has no business distinguishing one citizen from another by ethnicity, heritage, culture, religion or gender.

Yet a constitutionally enshrined 'Voice' will do exactly that. In addition, and as a conservative who is sceptical about governments' past track records in Indigenous Affairs, I am not convinced that 'more government', mandated constitutionally, will break the cycle of Indigenous disadvantage in remote communities. A 'Voice', however benevolent or sincere, will not guarantee integration, nor will it right the wrongs of the past.

The migrants who came to this country, particularly after the Great War, have never asked for a 'voice'; nor did they need one to achieve integration into Australian society. To overcome hardship and disadvantage, they committed their deeds and their determination to their new country. What mattered most was, in the words of Martin Luther King, Jr, the content of their character. This is a fundamental part of the great Australian success story.

Suggested Reading

Barnett, David (with Goward, Pru), *John Howard, Prime Minister* (Penguin, 1997).

Howard, John, *Lazarus Rising* (Harper Collins, 2010).

Iuliano, Susanna, *Vite Italiane: Italian lives in Western Australia* (UWA Publishing, 2010).

12

THE VOICE IN THE LIGHT OF THE WESTERN INTELLECTUAL TRADITION

Henry Ergas AO

That the proposals to enshrine an Indigenous assembly, referred to as "the voice," in the Australian Constitution raise many practical issues is well-known. Those include how eligibility to participate in the assembly, as a voter or a member, would be determined; what functions, privileges and obligations the body would have, as well as how those features of its status would be enforced; by what means it would be held accountable both to its constituents and to the Australian people as a whole; and what recourse the assembly itself, the groups it was intended to represent and other Australians would have to judicial review of its rules and operations.

So far, despite torrents of material that have been produced, almost always supporting the proposal, all of those issues remain clouded in uncertainty. But if a referendum on the proposal is to have democratic legitimacy, voters must know, at least in broad terms, what the consequences of their decision will be.

That much is stated with considerable clarity in the Venice

Commission's *Code for Democracy Through Law*, which is widely accepted internationally as the basis for assessing the quality of democratic institutions, including of electoral processes. Thus, as the Venice Commission has put it in its guidelines on referendums:

> The question put to the vote must be clear; it must not be misleading; it must not suggest an answer; *electors must be informed of the effects of the referendum*; voters must be able to answer the questions asked solely by yes, no or a blank vote [Code of Good Practice on Referendums (20 January 2009), my emphasis].

Indeed, one of the most common criticisms of the Brexit referendum was that the required information about the practical implications of the choices voters faced was not presented fully and fairly; were a referendum on the voice vulnerable to the same criticisms, the outcome would be durably tarnished and the integrity of our democratic institutions undermined.

Yet for all of their significance, the practical questions associated with the design of the voice are only a small part of the issues it raises. At the heart of the broader issues is the fact that it undercuts the core value of political equality, and in that respect reverses the arc of democratic progress. That trajectory involved progressively stripping away, or more properly, abstracting from, individual attributes such as parental status, wealth, religion, sex and race in determining membership in the political community; as those attributes ceased to be regarded as qualifications, ever broader groups of subjects became citizens, with the same rights to participate in the political process. By introducing indigeneity as a factor that determines political standing—and doing so in the Constitution, which is the nation's fundamental law—the proposal offends a deeply-held principle, with effects that include making Australia a nation that is ultimately less united and less able to overcome its differences.

In developing these themes, I begin by reviewing the role of the bedrock concept of political equality in the Western intellectual tradition and then link that concept to democratic political representation. On that basis, I examine some of the possible consequences of special, rather than equal, rights of political participation before drawing conclusions.

Political equality

Political equality is one of the most ancient and most fundamental values in the Western intellectual tradition. Although its substantive meaning, and intended scope, have changed over the centuries, the concept's origins can no doubt be found in the notion that man was created in God's image, where the Biblical notion of man is explicitly generic, eliding any specification in ethnic, religious or racial terms. And it is equally clear that the concept of human equality gained significant momentum first under the impetus of Pauline Christianity's universalism and then from the emergence in Scholasticism of the distinction between divine law, which could only be accessed through grace, and natural law which—as the canonists put it—was cognizable through a "faculty" or "power" implanted in human reason as such.

However, it was only in John Locke's later writings that the political implications of the belief that the reason which had been divinely implanted in all human beings gave them the capacity to understand the commands of natural law were made fully explicit. God, wrote Locke, created all of us in what was, morally speaking, "[a] state... of equality, wherein all the power and jurisdiction is reciprocal, no one having more

155

than another" [John Locke, *Two Treatises of Government, Second Treatise*: 4], all of us lords, all of us kings, each of us "equal to the greatest, and subject to no body" [*Second Treatise*: 123]. No matter how inadequate the average human intellect is for a

> ... universal, or perfect Comprehension, ... it yet secures their great Concernments, that they have Light enough to lead them to the Knowledge of their Maker, and the sight of their own Duties... It will be no Excuse to an idle and untoward Servant, who would not attend his Business by Candle-light, to plead that he had not broad Sun-shine. The Candle that is set up in us, shines bright enough for all our Purposes.

Now, Locke never denied that there were important distinctions in capacity among human beings, and hence in merit. On the contrary, he insisted on the point: "Though I have said above, Chap. II. That all Men by Nature are equal, I cannot be supposed to understand all sorts of Equality: Age or Virtue may give men a just Precedency: Excellency of Parts and Merit may place others above the Common Level" [*Second Treatise*: 54]. However, and crucially, Locke insisted that the differences were, in *political* terms, irrelevant:

> ... And yet all this consists with the Equality, which all Men are in, in respect of Jurisdiction or Dominion one over another; which was the Equality I there spoke of, as proper to the Business in hand, being that equal Right, that every Man hath, to his Natural Freedom, without being subjected to the Will or Authority of any other Man. [*Second Treatise*: 54]

In other words, Locke distinguished between the infinite variety, and individual uniqueness, of human beings on the one hand, and their fundamental and equal claim to dignity—and hence rights—on the other, thereby setting the foundations for modern liberalism.

Albeit through a long intellectual chain, that notion of an equal political claim then received a further important articulation through Hegel's distinction between the state and civil society. At the heart of that distinction was the division between the state, as the sphere of equality—where all citizens had the same rights and obligations under the law—and that of civil society, which "is the sphere... in which all individual characteristics, all aptitudes, and all accidents of birth and fortune are liberated" [G.W.F. Hegel *Elements of the Philosophy of Right*, 182 (A)].

Hegel fully realised that individuals differ enormously in their interests and abilities; and no one placed greater weight than he did on what he regarded as the distinctly modern urge for individuality to express itself, as it did in civil society. However, he also stressed, as no less distinctly modern, the equality that was being constructed by the progress of "abstract right", which would, in its full development, place citizens on a strictly equal footing. Overall, what made the modern world special was that it allowed both those tendencies—to equality and diversity— to play themselves out, with the first being the defining value in the political sphere, while the second operated in the sphere of "free association" (that is, of voluntary associative activity).

It was very much on those Lockean and Hegelian foundations that Hannah Arendt, writing in the wake of the Holocaust, elaborated her enormously influential approach to human rights. Equality, she said, was not the result of nature; it was born from the law, and notably from the law of democratic nations, which abstracted from all the fundamentally irrelevant differences between citizens—such as race—instead treating them all equally. As she put it:

> Equality, in contrast to all that is involved in mere existence, is not given us, but is the result of human organisation insofar as it is guided by the principle of justice. We are not born equal; we become equal as members of a group on the strength

of our decision to guarantee ourselves mutually equal rights. *Our political life rests on the assumption we can produce equality through organisation*, because man can act in and change and build a common world, together with his equals and only his equals [Hannah Arendt, *The Origins of Totalitarianism*, 301, my emphasis].

Nothing was more "alien" to that common world, Arendt argued, nor more fatal to its survival than allowing the "dark background of mere giveness, the background formed by our unchangeable and unique nature, [to] break into the political scene"—for "once its principle of legal equality has broken down ... the nation dissolves into an anarchic mass of over- and underprivileged individuals" [*The Origins of Totalitarianism*, 290].

Of course, none of that is intended to deny that the achievement of political equality was a slow process, marred by grave injustices and, at times, by terrible reversals. However, despite those delays and reversals, the steady enlargement of the circle of citizenship, which drew previously excluded groups into Hegel's sphere of "abstract right", has brought its full realization ever closer. And as Locke, Hegel and Arendt brilliantly stressed, it is by the extent to which they treat all citizens equally, according them the same political rights and obligations, that modern states must be judged.

In short, the essence of political equality is precisely that it sets aside individual attributes—such as ethnicity, descent, sex and religion—which may powerfully shape personal life but that are irrelevant to the rights and duties of citizenship. As it became a core value in the Western intellectual tradition, it gave strong impetus to the progressive extension of modern citizenship and the elimination of discrimination.

Representation

If political equality proved so powerful an idea, it was in large measure because it was intimately linked to equality of political representation, that is, to the principle that all citizens should have the same weight in the process of political decision-making.

Here too, the underlying abstract concept—representation and collective decision—is distinctive to the Western political tradition, and finds its roots in the Bible, most obviously in the notion of the collective covenant which bound the nation of Israel. But it also developed out of the Athenian democracy and the democratic elements in the Roman Republic. Particularly significant, in terms of the emergence of the contemporary concept of equal rights of participation, was the formulation in the Code of Justinian (elaborated in 529-534 AD) of the principle that *quod omnes similiter tangit ab omnibus comprobetur* ("what touches all similarly is to be approved by all"). With that principle being elevated into canon law in Gratian's 12th century Decretum, *quod omnes tangit* moved to the centre of constitutional law in the course of the 13th century, and by 1295 King Edward I of England was quoting it as the underlying justification for convening parliament.

Of course, merely invoking the principle that "what touches all similarly is to be approved by all" does nothing to precisely define the "all" that are to be represented. To some extent, the issue was addressed over the course of the centuries by the broadening of citizenship and of the rights it brought; but the difficulties and controversies associated with determining the contours and substance of representation and of participation in public decision-making went well beyond the issue of the franchise.

It was, in effect, by no means obvious that it was individuals who were being –or more properly should be—the focus of representation and the litmus test of its adequacy. Certainly, any such notion would have been entirely alien to the English tradition prior to the English Revolution; rather, in the late medieval and early modern world, the "balanced constitution" involved reproducing in the structure of political decision-making the organic and strictly hierarchical structure composed of the monarch and the estates. But even as late as the 19th century, the role of parliament as the "mirror" of the nation—or, in the words of James I, as an "epitome of the whole realm"—was viewed primarily in terms of ensuring a balanced representation not of individuals but of interests. Whether individuals had equal access to the legislature was neither here nor there; what mattered was whether the diverse interests that constituted society were adequately represented.

There were elements of that approach in Burke's defence of the unreformed suffrage, whose seemingly arbitrary and clearly unequal nature did not, he claimed, prevent it from yielding a parliament which was an "express image of the feelings of the nation" [Edmund Burke, *Thoughts on the Cause of the Present Discontents*, 118]. It was, however, the philosopher, historian, and MP James Mackintosh who in 1818 influentially advanced what later became known as the "variety of suffrages" theory of representation, which asserted that different groups merited different roles in the legislative process, broadly defined.

"To understand the principles of [the representative assembly's] composition thoroughly," Mackintosh wrote, "we must divide the people into classes, and examine the variety of local and professional interests of which the whole is composed." From the fact of that diversity, Mackintosh deduced that "the proper composition of the House of Commons," as well as "the justice of the government," entailed that "each of these [interests] must be represented", but not necessarily in the same way [James Mackintosh, "Universal Suffrage," *Edinburgh Review*, 31 (1818), 181, 175.]

As usual, it was the Victorian polymath Walter Bagehot who pushed this logic of collective rights to its logical conclusion. "To have a good Parliament," he wrote, "we must disfranchise some good constituents" by giving them fewer voting rights, so that their voice would not swamp those of potentially less vocal or otherwise more deserving groups [W. Bagehot "Parliamentary Reform", *Works* (1915 edition) III: 223].

While schemes which sought to put that approach into practice attracted considerable support in the great 19th century debates about representation, they failed at least in part because they seemed so inherently arbitrary.

For example, Albert Venn Dicey, the foremost constitutionalist of the late Victorian era, contrasted "a society such as that of the Middle Ages, where marked orders existed," with the England of his day in which social mobility—and the overlapping nature of social roles—meant that social groups were increasingly intermingled, to the point where "it had become absolutely impossible to draw a clearly marked line between the different divisions of the nation" [A. V. Dicey, *Essays on Reform* (1867) 74].

Equally, the towering moral and political philosopher Henry Sidgwick, while accepting that there might be "general considerations" supporting tailored forms of collective representation, concluded that "any scheme for applying them must necessarily be to a great extent arbitrary" [Henry Sidgwick, *The Elements of Politics* (1897) 377.] To that extent, they were every bit as irrational under modern conditions as the contention Locke famously mocked "that those who have black Hair or gray Eyes, should not enjoy the same Privileges as other Citizens " [John Locke, *A Letter Concerning Toleration*, 55].

Additionally, critics argued that any special form of representation—in which representatives were expected to act on behalf of particular groups or interests—would adversely affect the quality and integrity of the deliberative process.

Thus, John Stuart Mill, in bemoaning proposals for special representation, claimed that once representatives were attached to particular sections of the community, they inevitably became "mere attorneys of certain small knots and confederacies of men." Those "attorneys" would, by the nature of their role, focus on the narrow identity and interests of their section, making deliberation into what would now be called a "zero-sum game". And the hostility to other parts of the community that attitude implied would transform the process of reaching decisions into a battlefield of "private interests" [J.S. Mill, "The Rationale of Representation," *Collected Works*, XVIII: 44.]

Equally, Dicey warned that "incalculable evils" would flow from collective representation, as those who felt themselves to be "special representatives" of a designated group were disposed to believe that there was "something sacred" in defending their own group at all costs. They would, as a result, make the process of deliberation and decision one dominated by "the most fanatical, the most narrow" approaches, undermining every effort at reaching agreement [A. V. Dicey, "The Balance of Classes," *Essays on Reform*, 81].

In the end, however, what doomed these proposals was neither their practical difficulties nor their harmful consequences, significant as they were; it was that any concessions to collective representation—that is, to the representation of groups rather than individuals—grated so directly with the notion of equal, or liberal, citizenship.

Certainly, by the second half of the 20th century it was widely accepted that political equality required, in the words of two very distinguished scholars, that "the preferences of no one citizen are weighted more heavily than the preferences of any other citizen" [Robert A. Dahl and Charles E. Lindblom, *Politics, Economics, and Welfare* (1953), 41].

Moreover, the growth of executive government, and the expanding complexity of the public decision-making process, led to a broadening conception of what that principle meant. In particular, from being narrowly focussed on "one man, one vote" it moved to encompass the right to an equal role in the overall system by which political decisions were taken. Thus, as two other prominent commentators explained, political equality in modern democracies "means *an equal chance* for each member of the community to participate in the *total* decision-making process of the community", including in consultative and legal processes [Austin Ranney and Willmoore Kendall, *Democracy* (1956), 28]. Set against that standard, the notion that one group, and one group alone, would have special access to the legislative process seemed self-evidently at odds with the spirit of liberalism and the core virtues of a democratic society.

The return of collective representation

Nonetheless, by the 1980s, special forms of representation were back on the agenda. According to their proponents, their return was justified as a way of correcting under-representation— for example, of women or of racial minorities. Be it through quotas or by the definition of tailored electoral constituencies (notably the "majority minority" electorates the Supreme Court imposed on the US House of Representatives), those measures were viewed as an essentially transitory means of overcoming historical injustices; while they involved obvious departures from the principle of political equality, the departures were, at least in theory, intended to disappear once more equal outcomes had been achieved.

There was, however, an additional, and far more ambiguous, strand to the new wave of proposals. In essence, that strand breathed fresh life into the concept of "national minorities" which had played an important role in the system of treaties that came out of the First World War. The underlying notion was that even advanced societies contained enduring ethnic, linguistic or religious minorities; and that those minorities were entitled to permanent economic, social and political rights which distinguished them from the polity's majority group—rights which were codified, to varying degrees, in the minorities clauses of the post-World War I treaties.

As Hannah Arendt argued, those provisions almost invariably proved disastrous, doing far more to provoke public hostility against the designated minorities than to appease inter-community tensions. However, the notion of collective rights for national minorities—which had been elaborated even before World War I by the Austro-Marxists, and notably by Karl Renner and Otto Bauer—became a prominent feature of Communist rhetoric, with the Soviet Union claiming to have protected those rights through its system of ethnic and linguistic republics; indeed, it was mainly through the efforts of the Communist Party of Australia that proposals for "minority rights" and national self-determination for Indigenous groups emerged during the 1960s in the Australian civil rights movement.

As special representation returned to the agenda, new

international instruments—such as the Council of Europe's Framework Convention for the Protection of National Minorities (enacted in 2001)—reinvigorated those older claims for differentiated political rights, in both the advanced and developing countries. Bodies such as the Nordic countries' Sami Assemblies were hailed as a model; in the wake of gender and racial quotas, proposals for what were cast as merely consultative bodies seemed relatively harmless.

But the logic underpinning these bodies was never clear. It was, in particular, not apparent whether—like gender quotas— "Indigenous assemblies" were a corrective measure, which (at least in theory) would be unwound once some threshold of effective representation had been reached, or whether— like proposals for (say) greater federalism—they were a permanent change in structure of government and of political representation, accompanied by an equally permanent shift in the location of sovereignty. Nor was much attention paid to the likely consequences of creating and entrenching that kind of representative structure.

Yet the consequences of abandoning political equality were anything but trivial. No one stated them better than Harvard's Jane Mansbridge, who had been among the most prominent advocates of special forms of representation for disadvantaged groups.

Already in the late 19th century, Dicey had argued that instead of bringing into the legislative process the fact that the people being represented were "of different politics, pursue different professions and belong to different religious bodies", special forms of representation would throttle the richness of many voices into a single narrow voice.

Echoing, more than a century later, Dicey's concerns,

Mansbridge noted that "the diversity within historically disadvantaged groups is no less than in any other groups;" given that diversity, the consequence of special representation, which seeks to coax a unified view out of that plurality of interests and opinions, could only be "the suppression of [those] differences" [Jane Mansbridge, "Quota Problems", Politics (2005), 622 and follows].

At the same time, special representation was "fraught with danger" as it inculcates, both in the group itself and in the rest of the electorate, "the conviction that the individuals [who are being] represented have some essential traits that help define them and that render them unable to be represented adequately by those without such traits", breeding the very "essentialism" all genuine democrats have always decried.

And compounding the damage, the essentialism would act to "reinforce stereotypes, trap the individuals in the group in the images traditionally held of the group, deemphasize lines of division within groups to the advantage of dominant groups within the group, and harden lines of division between the disadvantaged group and other groups".

Given those effects, Mansbridge argued that any special forms of representation could only be justified as a temporary measure, which ought to be repealed as soon as "structural conditions improve"—that is, once the original under-representation had been corrected. They should therefore "be kept as flexible as possible", Mansbridge concluded, with their implementation "by voluntary adoption rather than by legislation, and by legislation rather than by constitutional mandate".

Conclusions

The contrast between all of these considerations and the proposed "Voice" could not be starker. Reduced to its essence, the proposal confers on Indigenous Australians—and on them alone—a constitutionally enforceable right to a formal consultative mechanism that would advise parliament on particular kinds of legislation.

In and of itself, that offends the core Western value of political equality, which requires that all citizens be given equal consideration, and equal means to participate, in public decision-making; and rather than build bridges between Indigenous and non-Indigenous Australians it seems likely to raise higher and more impenetrable walls. Moreover, as it entrenches those divisions, it will merely increase the pressures for even more extreme forms of separatism, fuelling demands for a formal treaty which would make Australia into some type of bi-national state.

Last but by no means least, far from respecting Mansbridge's recommendation for any form of special representation to be flexible and revocable, constitutional entrenchment means that once it is in place, reversing it would require a referendum which would inevitably be highly divisive.

There are, no doubt, policy decisions that are of special interest to Indigenous Australia—just as policy may have, and often does have, a disproportionate bearing on specific groups in the community. And it is equally undeniable that those most directly affected by a policy deserve to be consulted in its formulation. However, that is a right which should accrue, and largely already accrues, to all Australians, rather than being specially protected for one group alone.

That is all the more the case as the Australian community as a whole has an abiding interest in preserving and enhancing our shared sense of national identity; but the "voice" could alter the already fraught internal dynamics of our society—and not necessarily for the better.

It was, in effect, a crucial insight of early modern political philosophy, first powerfully articulated by Thomas Hobbes, that it is not "the people" that creates the institutions which represent its interests; it is instead the process of political participation itself which—by bringing citizens together in rituals such as elections and in the mechanisms for reaching public decisions—progressively forges society's disparate elements into a self-conscious "people".

And just as the fact of being equally represented, and of participating together in the periodic selection and assessment of our representatives, unites us, so separate representation could heighten everything that drives us apart, crystallizing the fault lines the proposal promised to repair. It is precisely with that risk in mind that Arendt—who could hardly be accused of being a reactionary—repeatedly stressed that the whole notion of separate and special representation is "contradictory to the very nature of [democratic] nation-states", to the point where the unified "nation state cannot exist once its principle of equality before the law has broken down" [*Origins of Totalitarianism*, 290].

The danger that the "voice" will lead us down that dark corridor on the basis of race—thus prolonging the sorry history of racial difference—merely underscores the need to subject it to careful scrutiny.

In exercising that scrutiny, it is worth remembering that the demand which resounded so loudly—and so successfully—with Australians in the 1967 constitutional referendum was for political equality, not for special rights. Nowhere was that emphasis on equal, rather than special, rights more eloquently captured than in the song which could be heard from one end of the country to the other during the 1967 referendum—a song exhorting Australians to "'Vote 'Yes' to give [Aborigines] rights just like me and you".

"The original Australians", insisted Faith Bandler—who came to embody the campaign's spirit—no longer wanted to be "a race apart in the land of their birth"; instead, the time had finally come for them to be "treated equally with other Australians".

It was therefore no accident that the demand, on the Indigenous petition which marked the campaign's origin, was not for the proposition that was eventually put to the Australian people—that is, an amendment extending to Aborigines the Commonwealth's power to make laws for any "race". Instead, it was for the deletion from the Constitution of all reference to race, cleansing our founding document of the stain which had tarred it from birth.

Unfortunately, that plea was rejected by the campaign's non-Indigenous advisers, who believed that special laws, passed using the race power, would eradicate Aboriginal poverty and hardship. Now, after decades of failure which should have shattered that illusion, we are once again being told that constitutionalising inequality will promote equality and that enshrining separateness will reinforce national unity.

In November 1965, when the proposal to extend the race power to Aborigines was put to cabinet, Robert Menzies demurred. "Shouldn't our overall objective be to treat the Aboriginal as on the same footing as all other Australians, with similar duties and similar rights?", he asked his colleagues. And wouldn't enacting "a separate body of laws relating exclusively to Aborigines" just perpetuate their treatment "as a race apart", making it even harder for the ultimate goal to be achieved?

That Menzies made many dreadful errors on Indigenous rights is a fact; but as his period in office was drawing to an end, he at least asked the right questions. So, once again, should we.

CONTRIBUTORS

Tony Abbott was the 28th Prime Minister of Australia

Janet Albrechtsen is a columnist at *The Australian*

Anthony Dillon is an academic and commentator on Aboriginal affairs

Caroline Di Russo is a lawyer, entrepreneur and commentator

Henry Ergas is a columnist at *The Australian*

Neenah Gray is a research assistant with the Indigenous Forum at the Centre for Independent Studies

Peter Kurti is Director of the Culture, Prosperity & Civil Society program at the Centre for Independent Studies

Rocco Loiacono is a legal academic, translator and writer

Chris Merritt is vice-president of the Rule of Law Institute of Australia

Nyunggai Warren Mundine is Director of the Indigenous Forum at the Centre for Independent Studies

Scott Prasser is a public policy analyst and commentator

Jacinta Price is Country Liberal Party Senator for the Northern Territory

Bernard Samuelson works in public policy

Amanda Stoker is a lawyer and was Senator for Queensland until 2022